Membership Site
MASTERS

STU McLAREN

Copyright © 2011 Stu McLaren

All rights reserved.

DEDICATION

This book is dedicated to the tens of thousands of WishList Member customers actively creating online communities and membership sites.

CONTENTS

1 **MASTER #1: The Prolific Veteran**   1
What does it take to create a 7-figure membership site? Find out from this master who with over 10 years experience, has had up to 48 membership sites running simultaneously!

2 **MASTER #2: The Freebie Genie**   25
Can you really get paid every month by giving the majority of your content away for FREE? The answer is YES as this membership site master shares his magic formula for blending both free and paid content en route to big success.

3 **MASTER #3: The Community Cultivator**   49
This master is proof that you can build a very profitable membership site even when working within a tiny niche market. With over 4,500+ paying members, you'll hear how to create a welcoming community that your members won't ever want to leave.

4 **MASTER #4: The Tester**   81
Flying in the face of conventional wisdom, this master marketer has built a 7-figure membership site by testing and tracking countless pricing and conversion strategies. You'll discover his highest converting tricks along with tips for maintaining an above average retention rate.

MASTER #1: THE PROLIFIC VETERAN

An Interview With Ryan Lee
From RyanLee.com

STU: Welcome Ladies and Gentlemen, my name is Stu McLaren, founder of WishList Member and I am very excited here today because we are going to be talking to somebody who has been running membership sites for over ten years. In fact, he had over 40 plus membership sites running simultaneously! He's had thousand of members, made millions of dollars, Ladies and Gentlemen please welcome Mr. Ryan Lee.

Ryan, how're you doing today buddy?

RYAN: Stu, my friend, I am so pumped to be here and I just wanted to say one thing, can I just say one thing? Stuuuuu – that's it, I start off every interview by saying Stu.

STU: Nice, Good branding, excellent.

Now Ryan, I am very excited to have you because, you and I are good friends, but beyond the friendship I have learned a tremendous amount from you when it comes to running successful membership sites. You've just got a wealth of experience, because as we said in the intro, you've been doing this for a long time. This is not something new to you. So, what first got you into building membership sites to begin with?

RYAN: This is kind of a brief history. My very first paid membership site was at the end of 2001, so its now been over 10 years. I had setup a free site before that and that's when I was still working full time in a children's rehab hospital. Then later on I was a Gym teacher and I set up a site just to put out some free articles about training and fitness, cause that's what I was doing.

At the time, I was training mostly athletes but I saw a couple of other people who were publishing information geared towards this market. That led me to a guy named Chad Packet (who I later become friends with) and he had a membership site in the general fitness and weight loss market.

After I saw his site I was like you know what, if he could do that for weight loss, I bet you I could easily do it with strength and conditioning, which is kind of a sub niche of weight loss and a sub niche of fitness.

So, fast forward, I launched my first membership site, and back then it was just purely as a way to supplement my income. I was working full time as a Gym teacher and I thought you know what, if I can make a couple thousand bucks a month doing what I love, that's gravy.

The first month out of the gate, I brought in just about six thousand bucks. I was like, Oh My Goodness. Don't forget back then in 2001, there was no You Tube and 80% of the people had dial up. Remember that? There was no audio, it was literally text articles and pictures that would take 10 minutes to download.

> "The first month out of the gate I brought in just about six thousand bucks"

So it was really old school. To collect payments I used Clickbank, and at that time had to use "yearly billing" because Clickbank 10 years ago, had no recurring monthly billing. So it was a very rudimentary site. I used FrontPage to build the site and everything was manually created. It was ugly but it worked.

As we are going to talk about over the next little while, I've learned a lot since then, but I've been doing it for a long time. I love membership sites and when you do it right, there is no better business in the world.

There is no better business where you can help people connect, build communities and make money month after month. I know I don't have to tell people about the benefits of membership sites, because everyone listening or reading to this has either bought WishList Member or has been a WishList client for a while, so they know the benefits, so lets just cut to the meat of this interview.

STU: It's an awesome story, because you started with your first membership site and then you went on a tear building multiple membership sites. I think this in and of itself is an important lesson for people to realize because you didn't just stop with your one strength and conditioning site. You really began to create all kinds of niche membership sites. Can you talk to us a little bit about that?

RYAN: Sure. A really important rule is to listen to what people want. When I built the strength and conditioning site, we had a forum and there was a lot of interaction. So I just started listening. I didn't guess what people wanted. But by listening, I started noticing pretty quickly there were a lot of questions geared towards "the <u>business</u>" of training.

"Listen To What People Want"

I thought initially I would get more coaches and athletes, but what ended up happening was I started getting a lot of personal trainers and strength and conditioning professionals. So they started saying "Ryan, how are you doing this while having a successful part time personal training business?"

So I started talking about it more and more, and people kept asking more of the business related questions. It wasn't long before I thought, "I bet this could be its own separate website."

That's when I did a lateral move by staying within that market but I gave them something different - another membership site that focused on the "business" of training.

Then on the strength and conditioning site more and more people started talking about "underground" type training (things like using kettle bells etc.). You gotta remember, this was like 10 years ago and although everyone knows about them now, back then it was new. That's when I recruited a guy to help create content for the site and I started a site called Underground Strength Coach.

All these other sites began just by listening to what people wanted. From there I built a membership site for 4 minutes workouts, then I launched a whole network of inner related fitness websites, and a whole bunch of others. Just listening to what people wanted but staying in that one market.

I didn't make the mistake of saying "Ok well, if I did well in the fitness market for memberships site, then I could do it for gardening. Then I could do it for hopscotch and auto mechanics as well."

I stayed in that one market and went deep. Without sounding arrogant, there was a time when I was the top guy in the fitness industry. I influenced a lot of people over the years, and it's because I was so focused on that one market. Now I've kind of moved away from that and gone to into the "general marketing" niche because that's where my passion is now.

"I stayed in that one market and went deep"

But here are a couple lessons from this:

1) Shut up and listen to what people want.
2) Give them what they want and be really, really focused on serving the market

If you do this, you'll be surprised at how many potential membership sites you can do within one market.

STU: Well I think it's a brilliant lesson for everybody because as you said, we often think if we have success in one market we can easily jump ship and start over in a brand new market. But, if you've built up so much momentum, then you'll have much greater success carrying that momentum forward from one site to the other within the same or related markets.

RYAN: Yeah it's a huge, huge mistake that I see a lot of marketers make. They have a specific skill and they start building a list in one market, and they think they should just jump over to a completely different market.

For example, if we were to relate this to the fitness industry again, let's say you get a trainer who has a really good system for reducing injuries. They're working with athletes to help them build strength. So they've built a list of 2000 athletes and coaches and a really good brand around helping athelets.

Then all of a sudden, this same trainer discovers that his massage techniques work well for seniors too, so he decides to create a site for rehabbing seniors. But while the same potential content may be a little bit different, you're now starting back at zero and now you have a list of zero seniors. Now you have to start over again and your athletes are wondering if you've forgotten about them. Now they're get pissed off and they end up leaving your original membership because they feel like you have left them.

The lesson is simple. Go in one market and say to yourself "I'm going to kick ass and I'm going to dominate and not going to settle for anything less."

Do not consider moving your markets or changing your direction until you are no. 1 in that market, because there's plenty to be made. I think it was Dan Kennedy who said "There's riches in Niches", and there really are.

STU: I want to talk about to about that a little bit further and then I'm going to shift gears and we'll talk about some other things.

Staying on that subject what advice would you have for somebody who's thinking about entering a particular market? Should they go general first, then look to build more specific niche sites after or do you suggest they start very niche and then broaden out after that?

RYAN: That is a great question Stu, and the reality is you can have arguments on both sides and have really good examples of success on both sides.

My personal opinion based on my experience and all the people I've coached is that I think your chances of success are much greater when you start really niched. You start with that big thing and you keep narrowing down and narrowing down until you're the no. 1 guy or girl in that market.

> "Your chances of success are much greater when you start really niched... keep narrowing down until you're the #1 guy or girl in that market"

A perfect example is my friend Perry Marshall. He could have gone into general online marketing. But instead of online marketing the sub niche of that is traffic. The sub niche of traffic is paid traffic. The sub niche of that is Adwords. So in this scenario, he went 3 o4 levels deep, found the sweet spot, and now he's the no. 1 guy in Adwords.

You can probably go down further than that. You could probably stay in the Google network and aim to be the no.1 guy for Google Content Network advertising or the no. 1 keyword guy. So you could position yourself so that all you talk about is keywords and everything about your business revolves around keywords. You could create software for keywords and membership sites for keywords because you're the keyword guy. Even saying this, I don't thing there's a keyword guy, at least if there is, no one comes to mind.

So in the fitness market, which I have done a lot of stuff in, you could narrow fitness down into all kinds of sub niches. There's weight loss, then there are specific types of weight loss. You could be the kettle bell guy for weight loss, or the kettle bell guy for women 35 and over who want to lose weight with kettle bells. So, drill down until you could be the no. 1 person and once you've become the no. 1 person, then you could look at expanding beyond that.

STU: I think it's a great piece of advice and the thing that I want everyone to hear is that you increase your chances of success. So you're not saying that this is the only way to go, but what you're saying is put the odds in your favor. Start with a niche market because its much easier to be a big fish in a smaller pond versus a big fish in a massive pond.

RYAN: Yes exactly, and if you really think about your potential customers sitting at the computer and they don t know you yet, there's a good chance that they might go to Google to find out more.

Using the example of the traffic expert, if they wanted to learn how to market online, they might type in a general keyword like internet marketing, if they do, good luck being no.1 in that or even being competitive as far as your search engine placement.

But if they're typing in something specific like Google Adwords or make money with Adwords, now they're looking for a specific problem to be solved. When you're focused on the niche market, your chances are so much greater. First, it will be much easier to get ranked high in the search engines for those specific terms and second, it will be much easier to convert someone to a subscriber and then eventually a paid customer.

STU: You mentioned in the beginning that you were using all kinds of different systems for your membership site and that you were trying to piece them all together, that it was cumbersome and wasn't easy – but you did make it happen. Looking back, how has your approach to building memberships sites changed over the years?

RYAN: Oh my gosh, it has changed tremendously. When I first started, I used Microsoft FrontPage and it was all hand coded and I would literally type in each page. To protect the content I used some kind of free password protection script. It was fine and did the job – but it certainly wasn't "easy". Then I hired some college kids to do some programming and it was a nightmare. The kid was never there, the site crashed and I tried to call him and his roommate answered the phone. It was just terrible. So none of that stuff was really working well so then I went to an upgraded solution. I ended up using a solution from one of our friends Tim Kerber, who's with Membergate, I used that for a number of years and it's been good. However now, I'm using WishList Member for any new site I create.

In 2007 I decided I wanted to use the WordPress platform to manage my content. That's when you guys came out with WishList Member in mid 2008 so I was quite a few years without it but I was a really early WishList customer and I liked it a lot. The only "snag" was that I had so many custom technical requirements that I began making things too complicated. So I tried a couple of different solutions, but now I'm back to WishList. What I love about it (besides working seamlessly with WordPress), is that once it's set up, my site is so easy for me to update. I literally go in, create a new post, and I click if I want to protect the post or not. Then it's done.

"For me now, it's about simplification"

For me now, it's about simplification. Simplifying my business and simplifying my life. I feel by using one simple format and one platform, something that's web based, I don't have to worry about the software downloads and all the headaches that come with trying to get too fancy or too technical. Plus, you guys provide great support and I'm just really happy with how quickly and easily I can get my membership sites up and running.

Also, I use Clickbank to process my credit cards and the fact that there is an integration within WishList Member for Clickbank makes the whole "business" side of managing a membership site even easier.

What I love about Clickbank is that they take care of 90% of our "accounting" stuff. They take care of refunds, they take care of billing and they take care of credit cards that are declined. They handle all the rebilling. They take care of affiliate tracking and paying affiliates so you don't have to worry about it. Affiliates love Clickbank because they are reliable and pay on time.

It's just such a relief to know that all that stuff is handled by someone else. It allows me to breathe and relax. I thank you guys for creating WishList and I thank the team over at Clickbank for making my life a whole lot easier!

STU: I appreciate all the kind words you said, but I want people listening to get the lesson of a tried and true "membership site veteran" because anytime that you can simplify the process of managing your membership site, you should! It frees up all kinds of time, energy and it relieves stress because now you can channel all that energy towards creating better content, focusing on your marketing and getting more signed up for your site. I think that is a big, big lesson for everybody.

We hear it quite often (in terms of Clickbank) and people say "Stu, I've heard you recommend integrating WishList with Clickbank, but they charge 10% of total sales."

My counter to that is "yes", you could find a cheaper processor in terms of doing it yourself and configuring it all yourself, but you've then got to worry about the management of the affiliate program, making sure affiliates are sent their checks, making sure the accounting is all handled etc etc etc.

When you take all of that into consideration, you realize that it really sucks your time away that could have been better spent focusing on creating better content and producing more effective marketing (the two things that will help you get more members).

I hope that people really grab that lesson from you because when it's coming from somebody who has made millions from membership sites, you can hear the sense of relief that Ryan has by simplifying the whole process down and just focusing on what he does best. Thank you for sharing that Ryan.

RYAN: People say that Clickbank takes a little bit more but let me just run through the numbers quickly, just to hammer home your point and you'll see why I'm such a big fan of Clickbank.

At the time of this conversation, Clickbank charges 7.5% for recurring transactions. If you were to go into your own merchant account (and I've done it every which way you could imagine), a typical merchant account is going to be 2.5 – 3%. So you're looking at a difference of 3 - 4.5%. But again, Clickbank does everything. They handle all the risk, they do rebilling, and you don't have to do anything regarding customer billing support.

You don't have to hunt people down for expired credit cards. You don't have to pay your affiliates. They handle all the tax stuff for your affiliates (and yes, they take care of all of that too!). Just that alone is easily worth the difference, plus the fact that if you're on Clickbank and you're within the network and marketplace, affiliates are going to find you automatically. So all it takes is one or two affiliates to find you and promote you and its well worth it.

I had my whole membership site last time working with a different platform, and I used my own merchant account and literally because it was such a nightmare, I basically told my techs to cancel everything. Cancel the entire inner circle. It was a lot of money, but I decided to start over and cancel it. I didn't want to deal with the nightmare of handling all that stuff again so I decided to start over and bring everyone in through my new site with WishList Member and Clickbank. It was a ballsy move but it's paid off.

STU: By simplifying your site I bet it has lifted a huge weight off of your shoulders and relieved a lot of stress. Because now your day is not being consumed by following up with people who's credit card hasn't gone through, or making sure affiliates are taken care of, or helping them get their links and stats and all of that.

Now you can focus on what you do best. I know as a customer of yours, you create kick ass content and the bottom line is the more we can have Ryan Lee creating more of that content, the better off we are as customers. So it serves not only you, because it simplifies your life, but it also serves your customers a lot better as well.

RYAN: Right, because then you can focus on the two things:

1) Focus on getting people in the door.
2) Focus on keeping them happy.

If 20 or 30% of your time is dealt with handling the garbage and the technical support or you're spending all the time and resources with billing, then you're taking away from one of those other 2 important components.

STU: I want to talk to you about something you just said there Ryan, because we've got a wide variety of people listening or reading this but what you said is relevant to everyone. We have people that are brand new to creating membership sites and we've got people who have a tremendous amount of experience with membership sites but here's what I like about what you said.

You really simplified something in your last statement when you said every membership site owner should focus on 2 things; getting people in and keeping them happy. Can you speak on those 2 things?

RYAN: Obviously you can have the best membership site in the world, but if nobody knows about it, you're not going to make any money.

So if you look at it from the really broad, thousand foot birds eye view, two things become obvious. Number 1 is you need to get people to your site. That means marketing, generating traffic, getting butts to the seats. And the good news/bad news is that there are a million different traffic tactics. What I recommend is you find the 1, 2, 3 maybe 4 different things that work, and just study them and go really deep rather than trying to implement 400 different things.

Find those couple of things that work to get traffic and just be the best at using them.

Some Of My Traffic Strategies Include:

1) Blogging - I blog consistently on my site which is also tied into my membership site. That gets me great search engine traffic.

2) Guest Blogging – This includes writing articles for other sites, or magazines.

3) Commenting on Discussion Forums – This is very simple but you'd be surprised at how effective it can be.

These are a few of the really simple things. But also, trying to also get some more online media doing interviews for other sites and especially joint venture partnerships.

So number one is you've got to generate traffic.

The second part of the equation is then keeping members happy. Stu I know you do a lot of training regarding member retention. There's a lot of retention strategies, tricks and tactics. But the reality is, keeping members really boils down to two basic strategies.

Keeping Members Really Boils Down To Two Basic Strategies:

1) Give Them Good Shit
2) Create Anticipation For Upcoming Content

First thing is you've got to give people good stuff. So if it's a content based membership site where you're providing articles, interviews, teleseminars, webinars or whatever the delivery system is, the stuff's got to be good. I don't care how many tricks you have, if your content isn't good, they're not going to stick around.

> "I don't care how many tricks you have, if your content isn't good, they are not going to stick around"

People look at their credit cards and it doesn't matter if you're charging $10 per month or $100 a month, they're going to look at it and wonder if it's worth it. If you don't have the goods, then go back to that, and deliver the goods.

Then when you're delivering the goods, you can start using some tactics. The easiest one is the cliffhanger. The two most powerful words by far for customer retention, member retention are "Coming Soon".

"The two most powerful words for customer retention are... Coming Soon."

So you just tell them what's coming next. Pick any market for a membership site – think of a market.

For example, let's run with the "gardening" example we had earlier. Pretend you write an article about gardening for your members and you say, "guys, next week we have a kick ass interview with a women who at home, has grown her roses to 15 feet using the secret ingredient that you could find at any health food store." Do you see how we've created anticipation for that one piece of content. Whatever your content is, get them excited!

If they even had the slightest urge to cancel their membership, now they'll be thinking "I was gong to cancel, but I want to see how she grew that 15 foot rose." So now they're going to stick around one more month. The bottom line is, give good stuff and tease the hell out of it.

Another example of this takes me back to my childhood. When I was a kid, I loved the show Dukes of Hazard. Do you remember that one?

Inevitably right before a commercial, there'd be a cliffhanger. Beau and Luke's car would be sliding across the ditch and the teaser would say something like "Are Beau and Luke going to make it? And is Boss Hog going to catch them?" Stay tuned. I was like "Oh my God… I've got to find out what happens!" That's what you want your membership site like. You want to have that feeling of "I cant go anywhere, cause I don't want to miss what's coming next week."

STU: Being a customer of yours Ryan, you also do a fabulous job of communicating with your members. A lot of membership site owners forget to communicate with their members. They just think that their members are going to come back and remember to check the membership site for new content. But the reality is they don't. S to counter that you have got to communicate with your members and you do a good job of giving them a reason why they should come back to the site again and again and again.

Can you talk to us about the importance of communication?

RYAN: There are two ways to look at membership sites.

One person I know (who is a very smart marketer) said you can just "set up the membership site and never contact your members again. And hopefully, they never see the charge on their credit card."

I personally think this is the absolute worst way to approach a membership site. I'd rather be in front of my members saying "Hey I've got good stuff to show you, and if you don't like it cancel, that's fine." But I'm not going to hide or hope that my members forget about the charges for my membership site. That's not the way I'm going to do it. I'm going to keep in touch with them often. Granted, you don't want to do it too much and you don't want to keep doing member updates every single day because there is definite point where the amount of content you deliver is overwhelming. And if people feel overwhelmed, they'll cancel.

> "If people feel overwhelmed, they'll cancel"

So you have to find that sweet spot for your list, your topic and your customers where it feels like they're getting a ton of value, but it's not overwhelming them. Even if you have so much content that you could do a new two-hour video every two days you've got to remember that people just can't consume that much. Then, if they start getting two or three months behind, they'll cancel.

Another real world example of this is with our supplement company. We have most of our people on auto ship but the most popular reason people cancel is because they don't take the vitamins and the pills, and they still have two bottles worth in their cupboard. So that's the point when they cancel. So, give them really good value, but don't overwhelm them.

For me, on members updates, I update the site once a week, and I tell them about it. But in terms of the general email, I also email four to five times a week with just other free content on my blog. The key reason is to show that I'm still here, I'm alive and I'm not going anywhere. I also use it as a way to position myself differently from my competition. The reason is because my competitors in the "internet marketing space" usually only contact their customers when they're trying to sell them something.

So I'm always giving them education and not just pitching them all the time. We've all had the experience of not hearing from someone for a long while and then all of a sudden they start sending you three of four emails in a row. You think to yourself "here we go, now all of a sudden they care about us cause they're going to try to start selling me something or launch something." In my opinion, this is such a crappy way to live and to market your products. I'm not trying to stand up and preach that I'm perfect, because I've screwed up more times than you can imagine and I'll continue to screw up on a daily basis, just ask my wife. But just try to do the right thing by staying in contact with your customers and continually deliver really good value without overwhelming them.

STU: I think it's a great piece of advice.

Now I want to shift gears a little and talk about your new site at www.RyanLee.com. On that site you do a great job of blending both free and paid content and I want to talk to you about that strategy you're using. We get asked a lot about whether someone should give away free content or should they keep it all behind a pay wall.

I personally think that there's a balance in that you can use the free content to draw attention to the paid content. Now the key I want everyone to notice is that you have both your free AND your paid content all on the same site. So when people go to www.RyanLee.com to consume the free content that you send out regularly they are simultaneously getting exposed to your paid content. Can you talk to us about that strategy?

RYAN: Yeah you hit it on the head. I put out a lot of free content and its probably 80-90% free content with the remaining 10-20% being my premium or paid content. For me the business is always changing and I'm always trying new things or different strategies.

> "I put out a lot of free content. It's probably 80-90% free content with the remaining 10-20% being my premium content"

Originally I put out two blog posts a day and I would make one free and one paid. The free post would be good but the paid one would be really "juicy". What I found was that I had to change this strategy because of a more selfish reason. I found after a while I was getting overwhelmed – it was getting hard to come up with the two new things a day so I was "forcing" content out that wasn't as good and the conversions began to drop.

So I went back to the drawing board and I asked a lot of questions. I wanted to get some feedback from my members and find out what my customers really wanted. What they wanted more than anything was more access to me. They wanted answers to their specific questions.

So I paired it down and decided to still give away a bunch of content for free. I give away tons of really good content including all kinds of articles and resources. But what you pay for are the weekly live trainings. So this setup puts a lot less pressure on me. I know that once per week, I'm doing the live training and it's going to be me answering questions. Sometimes I'll have special guests on with zero pitching. The rest of the stuff is the free content which I use to draw them in. Then when I do the replay and the live trainings I'll tease that within the free content and I'll make it it's own protective post too.

So the top part of the post (that everyone can see) will say something like "Hey guys training number two is up and you're going to see how to turn your blog into a SEO machine". Then the actual training is protected in the bottom part of the post. I'm always plugging the paid membership within the free content as well. For example I'll say "If you want to see this, don't forget our next training is coming within a day or an hour." So I draw them in with the free content and then I use that to get them into the paid part of the site.

STU: What I love about this approach is that it's an elegant way to use your content to generate interest in your paid membership. By using this approach the message is not coming across as a "hard sale". Therefore people are much more open to clicking through and consuming the free content. Then once you've got them there, the hope is that they'll say "you know what, this is really good stuff" and that's what's going to pull them into your paid content.

Another reason I like this approach is because it's a much easier way to sell your membership. Some people subscribe to the notice that you've got to sell, sell, sell. After a while, people just get turned off by always being "sold to" and then they become closed to the idea of clicking through and seeing your other stuff. So I've just found the strategy you're using a much more elegant way to use your content as a way to demonstrate the value you can provide and then incentivize them to come and join your paid membership.

RYAN: Yes exactly, and it felt better and more natural to me and I could see by the comments in the post that they appreciated it too. They appreciate not being sold all the time. If you don't want to buy, you can still come to my site all the time for really good free content, and that's fine. And you know what, you're going to tell people about it. So when they say "Oh have you heard of Ryan Lee?" they'll say "Oh my God his stuff is really good." As opposed to "I have no idea" because the only time he sends me emails is when he wants to sell me something.

If you think about it, at least in my space, how much content do you really see from other "gurus"? I say that because 99% of the time the only content you see is when they are trying to promote a product. So you don't really know anything about these "gurus". That's why I'm just trying to be different by opening up and providing ton of value. And to be honest, I really, really enjoy sitting down and creating these blog posts and this content. I love doing it and the fact that hundreds of thousands of people are reading this and it's helping to improve their lives, it just feels good. It's cool.

STU: As we continue to talk about your current membership site at www.RyanLee.com, I want to talk about a big change as you mentioned earlier in this interview.

You said that you were using another platform and it was getting complex and therefore creating stress as far as the merchant account and billing was concerned. So you made a pretty dramatic decision in that you said "we are stopping everything". I know you had a lot of paying members and you decided to stop everything and re-start it fresh on WishList and Clickbank. Can you talk to me about your thought process when you were making that decision and what can people now expect at the new www.RyanLee.com?

RYAN: My thought was everything was too chaotic. I was getting too many emails and having too many technical problems. Plus, I felt like the platform I was using was too limited, it wasn't user friendly. I had to do HTML stuff and it just wasn't working for me. When you add that on top of the shopping cart and the merchant account and the affiliates, it was just too crazy for me – remember I'm trying to simplify my life.

So I thought the site is bringing in good money, but I'm all about making my life easy. I'm married I have 4 young kids, I just want easy and simple. So I took a chance. I knew, because I had developed a good relationship with my members over the years that a large percentage would renew and rejoin again under Clickbank, and those who didn't – that's fine too.

That was my whole thought, just simplify. Knowing that it's on WishList, (a simple program that I can update it myself if I need to), I can now run the whole business by myself, knowing that Clickbank is taking care of the billing. So it just made sense. I knew I could get a lot of affiliates behind it, especially because it's Clickbank and they know that Clickbank takes care of payments and never misses a payment. All of that stuff made the decision easy.

So, it was just a simple, simple business model and in terms of what they expect, like I said, the biggest thing is that I first gave them access to pretty much all of my archive products. All the video's from my $2000 coaching program and all the audio's. There were hundreds of hours of content and a lot of great training (and that's just a bonus). The real meat of the membership is what is "happening now". These are live training calls every single week. No pitching. Just Q & A with special guests where we talk about what's working now.

You know how it is, you could buy a product today and two weeks it could be obsolete. You could buy a product about marketing with Facebook and Facebook could just do huge massive changes to their platform within a day or two and you think "now what"? The training is keeping you up to date about what's happening now, and its not every month like a lot of other marketers, or every other week, it's every single week. You are always going to get the freshest, latest stuff from me and I never sugar coat things. I will always tell you straight up how it is, or how I think it is. People appreciate that.

So life is great, I have a lot of members, people are loving it, they're spreading the word and it gives me more time to do interviews with people like you Mr. McLaren.

STU: I hope everybody can learn from your experience of moving to WishList in the fact that you identified that people want more of you. Ultimately, the easiest way for you to deliver that is through a once a week interactive coaching call where they can ask you questions and you can share what's happening right now.

When you have a membership site, the number one thing that people are coming to you for is convenience. Distilling information into the core essentials of what people need to know is a proven winner for membership site success. At the end of the day, people don't have the time to do all the research, they don't have the time to figure everything out and stay on top of it themselves and that's why they come to you.

> "When you have a membership site, the #1 thing that people are coming to you for is convenience"

I think that's a big part of why your site Ryan, is such a huge success. You do a great job of staying on top of things but then distilling it down and sharing it with your members in a much more intimate, much more personal nature.

RYAN: People want to connect and a mistake marketers make is thinking, "I'm just a solo entrepreneur with a membership site but I want people to think of my site as a huge company". Then they create some big generic corporate name like "Big Profits" and they never show who is really behind the site. Make it about you. Bring your personality into it and connect because people will stick with you when you deliver value and they see that you care. The bottom line is care, just care about your members and connect on that personal level.

"...people will stick with you when you deliver value and they see that you care."

STU: As we wrap up here Ryan, I'm going to give a recap for everybody else, but the final question I'm going to ask you at the end is, what advice you would have for other membership site owners? But before we get to that, let's take a look at some of the things we have talked about here today.

----- RYAN LEE INTERVIEW RECAP -----

So we've been talking to Ryan Lee, and as I mentioned at the top of this interview, Ryan has a tremendous wealth of experience when it comes to running successful membership sites. He's been doing it for over 10 years. At one time he had over 40+ membership sites running simultaneously. He's had thousand of members, made millions of dollars doing this stuff, so the guy knows his stuff.

The Beginning Of A Membership Empire

It all started back in 2001 when he began experimenting. He was publishing content on a free site for training fitness professionals, trainers and athletes showing them a whole bunch of different things he had learned in that industry. By doing this he noticed was that there was a lot of conversations around strength and conditioning.

So he spun that off and created a paid membership site on that very subject, strengthening and conditioning.

By creating this site, he was hoping to make some supplementary income to compliment his full time job as a teacher and the personal training he was doing on the side. His goal was to make about $2000 per month.

Right out of the gate, he made $6000 in his first month. This obviously turned him on to the concept of membership sites very, very quickly. But it wasn't an easy process because he had to bill yearly and the systems were very convoluted. The whole process of getting the sites up was a challenge, but he made it work. He knew right there and then that there was no better business to help people connect with one another and to make money.

Now if we fast-forward, Ryan is now in a position where he has got a ton of experience running successful membership sites and he's learned a thing or two. But the most important lesson for any membership site owner is to listen to what people want.

> "The most important lesson for any membership site owner is to listen to what people want"

Listen For What People Want

Even from the beginning, Ryan started noticing questions in his forum of his first site from trainers that were asking about Ryan's experience running a training business. They were more "business" related questions instead of specific fitness questions. Ryan then thought, "hey there's an opportunity".

From there Ryan made a lateral move and built another membership site focusing on the "business of training athletes". By monitoring questions from his members he quickly identified many opportunities for other membership sites and began rolling them out with "underground strength training" and then "4 minute workouts" and so on.

All these different, tightly focused niche membership sites, came as a result of listening to what people wanted. However, a key with this strategy as Ryan pointed out is to stay within the same market. Instead of trying to jump from market to market, Ryan said "stay in the same market and go deep". He said don't be afraid of spinning off another site but stay in the same market and go deep. When you do that you're able to carry that momentum from one site into the other. So listen to what people want, give them what they want and go deep in the market.

If you follow this advice, you'll dramatically improve your chances of success. Ryan said you can increase your odds even more by being very focused. Think about how the customer is going to search for information on that subject, and when you think about that, its much easier to target them and to convert them when you have a site that's very tightly focused.

Simplify Your Business

When Ryan started building his first membership site, it was all with things like Frontpage and he was a handing coding a lot of the site himself. Since that time he's moved through a variety of different systems and now uses WishList Member.

He has integrated WishList Member with Clickbank and one of the primary reasons he uses Clickbank is because it simplifies his business and his life. Now he doesn't have to worry about the accounting and the affiliate side of the business along with all the things associated with processing money - because Clickbank handles all of that. Combine that with the fact that WishList Member has given him the ability to easily publish content and protect it with one click, the process of creating a winning membership site is much easier than when Ryan began.

The 2 Keys To Membership Site Success

Ryan said the key to membership site success boils down to two simple things that all membership site owners should focus on.

1) Getting more members into the membership
2) Keeping those members happy.

When it comes to getting more people into your membership that always boils down to getting traffic (eyeballs) to your site so people actually see what you have to offer. It's all about your marketing.

Ryan suggested implementing 4 – 5 traffic strategies that work for you. Everybody is going to be different and there are going to be different marketing strategies that will be more appropriate to you but just focus on 4 – 5. Don't try to do everything. Just get really good at those 4 – 5 things.

For him, blogging is one thing that works really well. It helps with search engine optimization and it helps to get eyeballs to his content. He also guest blogs, publishes articles, conducts interviews and participates in various joint ventures. Those are the core things he does in his business, but he said whatever you're doing in your business, just focus on 4 – 5 strategies.

Then when it comes to keeping people happy, he said always give them good stuff. That's the bottom line that all membership owners should focus on, give your members awesome content.

The other thing that works really well when it comes to retention are two powerful words: "coming soon". You've got to create anticipation for your content. Create anticipation for what's coming up so that people have something to look forward to. Always communicate and always keep them anticipating what's coming up.

Old School vs. New School Membership Sites

Ryan went on to say that there are two ways to look at membership sites. The old school of thought is to set up a membership site, don't communicate with your members and hope that they forget they're getting billed. But the new school of thought, the one that Ryan subscribes to, is to keep your members informed of the value that they are receiving and communicate with them on a regular basis.

With that in mind, he said that you don't want to overwhelm your members, because if you overwhelm them by giving them so much content that they can't consume it, even if you're communicating all the time, your members are going to feel like they're not getting the value that is being delivered and they will therefore cancel.

Ryan likes to adhere to a once a week update, where he updates his members on all the things that have been happening and then he communicates regularly throughout the week by giving them free content and goodies.

Balancing Free vs. Paid Content

When it comes to free and paid content, Ryan said 80-90% of his content that he publishes is actually free. He uses it to drive people to his membership site where the paid content is located. It's all contained and located on the same site and that's really one of the big benefits of WishList Member. You can pick and chose which content you want available for free and what content you want to protect.

Ryan publishes a lot of regular articles where people can take that information and be able to apply it on their own. He said the paid content is really access to Ryan. Basically it's Ryan distilling a lot of information down to the nuts and bolts for his members, giving them practical how to's and showing them what they should be doing in their particular business.

He uses the free content to generate interest in the paid membership and by doing this, he's noticed an increase in comments as well as a lot more people appreciating him for the free content. The result of this is that it's generated more word of mouth and more sign ups.

Starting Over

Ryan also recently made a big shift with his main membership site located at www.RyanLee.com. He completely overhauled the entire site and in fact even though he had lots and lots of paying members, he shut it all down and moved to WishList member and Clickbank. The reason; to simplify his life. He said "I had a good relationship with my members, so I knew a lot of them would sign up again. Some didn't and that's ok." Doing this has given Ryan a simplified breath of fresh air where he can now focus on what he does best and that's creating kick butt content and cranking out top quality marketing material.

Tips On Building "Community"

As far as the "community" aspect of running a membership site, Ryan said the main thing to realize with the membership site is that people want to connect. A big mistake that a lot of people make is that they try to position themselves as this "big company". Forget that, be you, show that you care, show that you connect with your members and continue to deliver great value and you'll have a very successful membership.

----- END OF THE INTERVIEW RECAP -----

STU: Ryan, there is so much goodness contained in this interview and as I was going back through what we covered, I was thinking this is really good stuff.

The final question I wanted to ask you is what advice would you have for other membership site owners, who are perhaps not experiencing the kind of success that they really want to or someone that is staring for the very first time?

RYAN: I would say the first thing you have to do is look within yourself and ask yourself how badly do you really want it?

We can give you all the tactics and strategies and all that stuff, but unless you really want it, you won't do what's necessary to achieve it. If you look at the most successful people in the world, they tend to be the most driven. They're the ones who are the most hungry. So ask yourself how badly do you really want it? If you really want it, then go for it and cut the excuses out because everyone's good at making excuses.

> **"Don't tell me you don't have time.**
> **You have to make time."**

Don't tell me you don't have time. You have to make time. You can carve out an hour a day, everyone can. Stop watching so much TV. Stop doing all those other things. Look in the mirror and take 100% responsibility for everything you have. That's getting a little hard core but it' absolutely true. I'm not some motivational speaker here – but it's the truth.

The second thing is finding that niche or place where you can become the instant expert. The place where you can make a splash big time.

Finally, have the confidence to go after your goals and don't stop until you reach them. That's it.

I could have repeated myself with things that were said in the interview, but I don't want to sound repetitive. It really is a lot of the stuff that we have been talking about today. Implement those tactics along with the hunger and your goal list.

STU: Ryan I want to thank you. I know you did this as a favour, because we're good friends. There is just so much knowledge contained in that cranium of yours after running so many membership sites over the years and we appreciate you openly sharing it with all of us.

RYAN: Anything for you Stu, I'm just glad to help and I look forward to hearing all the success stories, and welcoming every single listener to the new inner circle.

STU: I would encourage and invite everyone to go and check out Ryan's site as there is a lot of free content and you'll also see what he's doing from a marketing perspective as you'll see how he encourages his members to sign up for his inner circle.

Profile Information

Name: Ryan Lee
Website: www.RyanLee.com

The Prolific Veteran

MASTER #2 – THE FREEBIE GENIE

An Interview With Andrew Warner From Mixergy.com

STU: Welcome ladies and gentleman. My name is Stu McLaren, co-founder of WishList Member and I want to welcome you to today's interview where we will be speaking to Andrew Warner, the founder of Mixergy.com.

Now Andrew's had a ton of success in business and one of things that he wanted to do was distil that knowledge by not only sharing his thoughts on business, but also the thoughts of many other successful business owners as well. Today, he does that through his site Mixergy.com.

So with that, welcome Andrew.

ANDREW: Thanks for having me on. I've gotten so much out of listening to your interviews with other people and I'm glad that I am going to get the chance to contribute back by sharing what I've learned.

STU: Well I'm just very excited because you're like the Larry King of the digital world and this is just going be a great interview. I can't wait to dig in.

So what I want do is I really drill down into the success of your site. I want talk to you about what you're doing because Mixergy.com is a great example of a membership site that combines both free and paid content. I want talk to you about how you manage that as well as how you made the transition to finally offering paid content. I also want talk to you about some of the other little tips and tricks that you are utilizing within your site.

So before we get started can you give everybody a thirty second overview of what is Mixergy.com?

ANDREW: Mixergy is a website where I interview entrepreneurs about how they built their business. And when you say I'm the interview king I'm not sure that I've gotten to Larry King's number of interviews, but I have 614 interviews on the website with people like the founders of Wikipedia, Kiva, Groupon, LivingSocial and many more. All these great people have come on and let me interview them about how they built their businesses.

I offer those interviews for free for a week or two and then we move it to our "members only" content so that people have to sign up and pay the monthly membership fee in order to access all the archived interviews and content.

We also recently added courses where I bring back many of these entrepreneurs and I say: "Show me your computer screen and teach me one thing that you do well".

So if you're really good at SEO, teach me how to do search engine optimization. If you're really good at building membership sites, which, Stu, you are, and I invited you to come on and teach me and my audience how you do it. That was a course that is only available to our members and we get people to sign up to take those courses and listen to old interviews.

STU: Now I want to dig deep here because Mixergy in the beginning didn't always have paid content. When I first saw it, everything was free. What was your strategy with the old site? How did you make money when you were giving away all of your content like that?

ANDREW: I wasn't really. And then when I started charging I got a bigger audience and I started bringing in more revenue. And I'll tell your audience how I did it, as much as I can. And I'm willing to be open but I think if they go to the site and spy on me, they're going to discover many more tactics than I could even reveal in this interview.

> "When I started charging, I got a bigger audience and I started bringing in more revenue"

I also think if you sign up to the mailing list of anyone who comes on here to do an interview, and you spy on their websites and you guys are going to learn even more.

But in the beginning of Mixergy.com, I wasn't making money. I was selling advertising. Then, I discovered WishList Member and I installed the plug-in myself and started using it. From that point forward, like I said, the audience grew, the revenue grew, and we had a whole new revenue stream.

STU: So in the beginning you were supplementing your site and your time by selling advertising. I know you do that during your interviews with the sponsors you mention during your introductions.

Then, when you made the transition to paid content, you immediately added another revenue source. Can you talk to me about the difference that made for you in terms of having more income to be able to do more things?

ANDREW: I decided when I launched the site that I wouldn't put any of my own money into it at all. Obviously for something like this there's no venture capital. My thought was, I will just let the site survive or die on its own.

And the money from advertising was doing okay but when I started charging I brought in even more money. This enabled me to hire an editor to edit my interviews, a course producer to talk to people and help them work through their courses to make them as useful as possible. I now have someone to be a pre-interviewer and a researcher.

So because of the people I've hired, the work has gotten better and better. That is directly attributed to the revenue that's come in from charging for the monthly membership.

STU: You mentioned that by transitioning to a paid content site your revenue grew (which we just talked about), but your audience also grew as well? Is that right?

ANDREW: Yeah absolutely. So here's how the audience grew.

"I create a sense of urgency that gets people to take action and go watch my interviews quickly"

By telling people that the content is free today but a week from now you're going to have to pay, I create a sense of urgency that gets them to take action and go and watch those interviews quickly.

And I've tested this in the emails that I send. I will send out an A/B test. In one email I say "this is going to be free for a week". In the next email I say "hey go and watch this interview", without mentioning that it won't be free after any period of time. When I say it's free for a short period of time, more people click, more people go and watch, more people go and download.

> "When I say it's free for a short period of time, more people click, more people go and watch, more people go and download."

The problem with blogs and interviews and any content online is that there's no sense of urgency. Why would anyone go to your website right now and download, watch it or read it? There just isn't a reason for it. And so if you create the sense of urgency they have to.

STU: I think this is a really powerful lesson for anybody who is publishing content, whether it be free or paid, because you hit the nail right on the head - especially with free content that you're giving away. When there's no urgency, people will put it on the 'I'll read that later' list. In fact, I've got one of those lists, where I see articles that I know I'll be interested in but I just don't have time at that particular moment. And inevitably I say to myself, "I'll read that later".

Unfortunately that list grows and grows every day and I very rarely get back to actually reading some of those articles. So this is a great strategy to encourage people to consume your content, and when they consume it, that's when they get value and they appreciate the site more. Would you agree?

ANDREW: Absolutely. And also if you put a price on it, it doesn't seem like another free piece of content that's available online. When you value your content enough to charge for it, the audience values it enough to want it and to ask for it.

"When you value your content enough to charge for it, your audience values it enough to want it"

I used to have older interviews on the website, and because they were older, people just wouldn't watch them. I saw the traffic numbers. They were junk. I would even promote it by putting a big picture of the person who I interviewed two months ago on the home page and still people wouldn't click because it's an old interview. No one wants old.

But once I started charging, people started begging me for old interviews. If they couldn't afford them they would email me and say "Andrew, I can't pay $25 a month" – which really, how can you not have $25 to just go and watch this? But fine. They'd say "I can't afford to watch it. What do I do to get it?" And I'd give it to them. But that fact is they value it enough to ask for it. I shows that we have been able to turn "older stuff" that people didn't value into valuable property.

STU: Well, I love what you've done with it and I'm so glad that you are charging for it because to me, it's just a huge well of information that people can go to time and time again. There are some kick-ass interviews on that site. Personally, I've made a habit of listening to them every day when I'm walking the dog. That's pretty much my daily routine.

Moving on, I want to talk about how you structured your paid content. When you made the transition to paid content you said you were using WishList Member. I want talk to you about how you're setting this up because now you are also offering courses. So first, let's talk about the courses and let's dig a little deeper there. Then I want to talk to you about the behind the scenes set up so people can get an idea of what you're doing.

So on your site you have over 600 high quality interviews which are available for free during the first week that you post them. Then you archive them and they go into the paid area. You also have courses that you offer on the site. Can you talk to us about what those are and where the inspiration for those came?

ANDREW: Sure. The interviews happen via video Skype and we just show the two videos (my video and my guest's video) as we talk to each other.

The courses we add another element. We show the guest's computer screen and if he or she is going to talk about SEO, we say don't just talk about how to do it, show us.

For example, we'll ask them to bring up a WordPress site, then go into the backend and show us which plug-ins we need to install. We ask them to show

The Freebie Genie

us how you install those plug-ins, explain why you chose those plug-ins specifically for increasing search engine optimization, show us maybe traffic numbers of how each one of those plug-ins helped you get more people to your website. Basically we ask our guests to walk me through and teach me how I can do the same thing. I want the specific details right down to installing a plug-in, setting it up exactly right, and then teaching me the ideas behind using it.

And that's essentially what makes up one of our courses. We do that using GoToMeeting. With GoToMeeting we can show my face as I talk and my guest's face as he or she talks, plus we can also show their computer screen.

STU: So did the idea for this come from feedback from your audience who were asking for follow-up on some interviews? Where did the idea come from?

ANDREW: It came from people saying make it even more practical and more useful. I try to make my interviews not just conversations but I try to pack as many tactics as possible into them. And I want to know specifically how each guest used those tactics.

So, for example, the founder of Groupon, I don't want him to just say "Start off simply". I want him to explain how he set up a WordPress site to launch Groupon and how he got his first users and his first customers and so on.

Well, I tried that and people said "We want even more. We like it and we want even more". And I wasn't sure what they had in mind so I tested via email an idea for a course. I said, "I'm thinking of doing a course on the site. I'm not sure which topic it'll be. If you want sign up, I'm only going to accept twenty people. Click here and just tell me a little bit about why you want to sign up. Plus, tell me which of these topics do you want sign up for".

Inevitably I got a lot more people signing up for it than I expected and the topic that they mostly wanted to learn was how to launch their product or business. So I thought alright, let's put on a class on how to launch. I'll have a friend come in and he'll teach it.

And that did pretty well, even though the technology was crap. We had all these issues with the audio and the video and everything went bad and yet, it still did pretty well. So I thought, you know, let's try again. And let's try again. And again and again and again. And I fell in love with doing them because I'm a curious person. I want to learn this stuff myself.

For example, when I had you on to teach how to do membership sites, it wasn't just because it was going to sell to my audience. In fact, the primary reason I did it was I'm curious. How do I build a better membership site? And I know if I'm curious about it, there will be other people who are curious and want to learn too. And if I'm curious and I want specific information that I can use, then I know I'll be able to get specific information that my audience can use. And it was as simple as that.

STU: One of the things I hope people get from that response, Andrew, is your willingness to try different things. I love hearing about how you went through that process because, you know, a lot of people are afraid to try new things with their membership site or with their email list. They just aren't willing to experiment with making things better. But for you, this was a chance to test a hunch, an idea, that you thought might work with your audience. You sent out an email but you were just testing the waters. And based on that response you made progress from there.

> "One of the things I hope people get from that response is your willingness to try different things"

The other thing I hope they get is the fact that the first course you did wasn't perfect the first time you did it. In fact, you said a lot of things went wrong. But that didn't discourage you from doing it again. Can you talk to us a little bit about how things continuously improve with not only your interviews but your courses?

ANDREW: Yeah. The way that we improve – the way I personally improve – is by not worrying excessively about quality but by being obsessed with quantity. And I know that this isn't a popular point of view but I'll explain it.

"The way we improve is not by worrying excessively about quality but by being obsessed with quantity"

If I sit down and think about like how do I ask the right question? I'll take two months between interviews or even one month between an interview. By doing that, I'm just not going to improve. I'm going to obsess and I'm going to hold myself back.

But if I say to myself "I'm going do an interview every day. I'll just publish it every single day and if it's bad I'll publish it and if it's great I'll publish it, but I'll force myself to produce". With that production schedule if I screw up on Monday I can't escape the screw-up on Tuesday. I can't procrastinate. I can't keep from learning from the mistake because I've got an interview on Tuesday. So whatever mistake I made on Monday, I know I've got to get it a little bit better on Tuesday or else I'm going to suffer again from the insecurity of publishing something bad. And so I just keep publishing and publishing and publishing. And with that, I get better and better and better. And I just look for small changes that I can make to improve.

"I just look for small changes that I can make to improve."

So, for example, if I see in one interview that a guest is rambling and I didn't pull him back, I'll publish that anyway. Often I think it's rambling and the audience says hey, this is still a great interview. So that's one reason why I publish it regardless of the mistake I see. But the other reason I publish it is because the next day when I see someone's going a little bit too far (or rambling), I'll say "forgive me, I want hear more about this story but I've got to ask you about this other thing here too or else I'll really be in trouble with my audience if I don't push you on that".

And so I practice that. And if that doesn't work then I come in with another approach the next day. Each time I conduct an interview I'm just looking to improve one small thing.

STU: So you get better by doing rather than obsessing over planning or making a mistake beforehand?

ANDREW: Yeah, exactly. And the internet is so good for allowing you to just keep putting stuff out there. By doing so, people just find you. The more stuff you put out there, even if it's not your best stuff works to help you attract an audience. Google doesn't know that it's not your best stuff. So everything you publish is another Google hit. Let me give you an example of that.

I did an interview with the founder of Sex.com. I'm not sure it was my best interview but it was pretty good. I still get hits from people who type in the word 'sex.com'. I don't know why but they type it into Google but inevitably they discover my site as one of the search engine results and a lot of them click over to my site.

I get people finding old interviews that I don't think are especially good.

Here's another example. When people type into Google 'I hate you', the same thing happens. I did an interview with someone who got inspired when he got a note on his car randomly that wasn't meant for him. It said 'I hate you' and he talked about that in the interview.

I guess that was in the transcript because I still get traffic from the phrase 'I hate you'. Even though it wasn't one of my best interviews, it's still out there generating traffic for my site. People come because they type in 'I hate you' randomly into Google and they land on that page. They either the interview or they click over to another post on the site. That's when I've got them.

Regardless of whether it's "bad content", it's still content that could potentially get you new customers and new visitors.

STU: I love it. As we move forward, I want to talk to you about how you first created a lot of content before you transitioned to a paid membership site. Initially you really used your content to build your audience and to create a following.

Can you talk to us about making the transition from free to paid content and what that was like for you?

ANDREW: To be honest with you, it was pretty rough. I got beaten up a lot online for doing that. And because of that I thought about the way that I transitioned and I realized I should have just charged for something right from the start.

> "I realized I should have just charged for something right from the start"

I should have let people know that this is a site that cares about making money. I should have done that, because of the kind of people who I'm going after are real cutting edge, start-up-oriented tech guys. But they're not used to paying for anything. They just want free, free, free, free, free.

Because of that, I got screwed. The message boards which sent me the most of my traffic are the ones on Hacker News and the people there started ripping into me when I went to a paid membership model. Thankfully, there were a few people who also understood that more revenue meant I could turn this into a real business. That mean I could actually hire people and improve the quality of my work. Also if I'm talking about entrepreneurship and I don't charge, it means I don't understand the first thing about business. And so, I have to charge. So other people began saying this on my behalf in the message boards and that helped out a lot. If I could do it again though, I would charge as soon as possible.

STU: And that's interesting to hear, because I think that's a huge challenge for some people. People are always scared to begin charging for content. They wonder whether people will pay. And in this situation it was an even bigger challenge for you because you had essentially trained your audience to expect everything for free.

ANDREW: Yeah.

STU: And now that they are trained to expect everything for free, making the transition to paid content becomes an even bigger hurdle.

ANDREW: If I could do it again, I would ideally start charging for the older interviews or start charging for something from the beginning and let people know that I'm going to adjust.

Having said that, if I didn't do that and it was time for me to charge, I would probably not charge for the stuff that was already free. I would probably add something else and charge for that. And then maybe slowly go back and charge for the stuff that was free. But to just right away start charging for stuff that's already free is a shock for people and it also keeps them from understanding the business model because some people had a hard time making the distinction between the limited availability of the free stuff and when it got moved into the paid archives.

So if I were doing this again, I would charge right from the beginning if I could. If I didn't do that and I already had free stuff on the site, I would charge for some new thing and then I would slowly expand what I was charging for and the quality of it.

"Initially I would not obsess about making it good. Just put it out there."

With that said, the one thing I think is important for your audience to hear is that initially, I would not obsess about making it good. I would just put out there…even if it's a piece of garbage. It's okay, you can charge for it and then when you improve you can give the new free thing to your audience later on when you get it better. Or, you can charge for it, get money and then give a refund right away. But you've got to learn, charging for stuff is a skill. It takes time. I didn't learn how to write the right sales page right away. I didn't want to. I didn't want to "hide" while I built up the perfect product and the perfect site so that I could start charging. I wanted to learn slowly how to do it and okay to learn it in public. And it's okay, I think, to tell people that I'm not going get it right the first time. You should expect that I'm going to learn in public and make mistakes in public.

STU: That's a big, big lesson for everybody. People want to make it perfect and inevitably, they never get it going. As you stated, you learn the most by "doing" and that's really where you're going make the most progress.

So let's talk about that. As we've seen on your site, you do experiment with a number of different ideas. And one of the things that I find very clever about Mixergy.com is how you draw people in with your free content, as we talked about, by creating urgency (ie. it's only going be free for a certain period of time). But inevitably when people are on your site they're going be clicking around and looking at other interviews. And when they do, they can see the content but they just can't access it. Is that using some of the protection features of WishList Member?

ANDREW: Yeah, absolutely. WishList enables me to hide content from people who don't have the membership level that entitles them to view that content. And then it allows me to put up an image in place of that content.

Here's what I do. I make old videos and MP3s only available to two membership levels: "Premium" and "Vault". If you don't belong to one of those levels, I hide the content and instead I put a picture that looks like a video player with what looks like a big "PLAY" button on it. This encourages you to click on it because it looks like you've got this video that you're about to watch. However, when you click on it, instead of the video playing you're taken to a page that says "you have to pay or log in if you want to view the video".

I want people to at least say to themselves (and to me) that "I want to watch this". And if they say to themselves "I want to watch this" and then they see a page that sells what they want, they then at this point just have to decide do I want to pay for it or not?

> "If I said right away that 'this video is only for members', people wouldn't even consider it"

If I said right away "This video is only for members", people just wouldn't even consider it. They wouldn't think about whether they should hit PLAY or not.

STU: I think it goes back to when we were kids. We always want what we can't have or what we're told we can't have! And in this situation you've created desire and people are clicking through to listen to those old interviews. However, you're intelligently using the non-member redirect to send them to a page that says "This is archive content. It's part of the premium membership. Here's how you can sign up".

It's just a beautiful and elegant example of how to utilize some of the features built into WishList Member to create interest in the content, still protect it, and yet also drive them to the place where they can then purchase it and begin accessing.

I highly encourage people to go to Mixergy.com and just go back a couple of pages and try to access one of the old interviews. You'll see this strategy in action. It's just a great example of how to use the features built into WishList Member and drive non-members to a place where they can actually pay.

Now based on that, how has this process impacted your sales? You mentioned you tried a number of different things and now I see that you've settled on the "video player" image. Was that the clear-cut winner for you in terms of conversion?

ANDREW: Well to be honest I'm not doing a lot of A/B testing on that anymore. I just settled on that. It works okay and I'm happy with it. Because in addition to also getting more members that way I am also able to see what videos that people aren't interested in.

I want to know what's sending more people into the membership paid page so I get a sense of which kinds of interviews people value enough to want to "play". This helps me get a sense of which interviews get people to pay to join the membership.

So I get a little bit of data from that and I've played a little bit with improving those click-through rates, but then I stopped and moved on to other areas of the site.

As I looked at the questions that you sent me in preparation for this, I realize, you know, there's a lot that we could be doing better. And I started to beat myself up and say "Why aren't we testing that image? Why aren't we doing this?". I realize, no, weren't not doing it because I can't do everything. I have to focus on a handful of things and do them well. And what's great about the model that we have (that you guys enable us to have), is it's a membership model. I just need to get my members to stick with me from month to month to month. And in time I'll improve more and get other things right and they'll be there to experience it.

> "I can't do everything. I have to focus on a handful of things and do them well"

"Every single month we made more money than the month before... that's one of the reasons why I really like having a membership program."

And what's great about the membership model is that even at my worst (and we've screwed up in the past with the way that we launched the membership and the way that we sold it and so on), even with our bad days and bad months, every single month we made more money than the month before. Every single month the revenue has grown with membership. And that's one of the reasons why I really like having a membership program.

STU: So talk to me about this, Andrew, because you mentioned you have two different membership levels. So let's talk about the "technical" aspect of that. You said you had a "Premium" level and you had a "Vault" level. Can you explain to us the difference between the two and is there a difference in price point of those two levels?

ANDREW: Yeah, I'm actually not selling the Vault level. The Vault is only the old interviews. It's the 600-plus interviews that are available only to members. Premium contains those interviews plus all the courses. And that's what I sell: access to Premium.

I have another strategy with the Vault level. I realized once I put a price on my content, I immediately gave it value. And so now I've got this valuable asset that I've created, because there's a price on it. And if there's someone who I want to work with, I can give them this valuable thing that I've created that has a price on it. So we send out volunteer requests for certain things on the site. And what we do instead of paying people is say "You'll get access to the Vault".

I also get emails from people who say "I want access to those old interviews but I can't afford them". And I say "alright, great, I'll give you the Vault. Can you help out one of my guys who's trying to help out our audience?".

Now that we've created this asset, I'm constantly thinking of other ways to use that asset (the Vault). Now that we have the Vault, I'm always trying to think of creative ways to use it.

STU: I love it! I'm taking notes on that one Andrew because I think that's a brilliant strategy to combat the people who do want to have access to your site but for whatever reason can't find the money to be able to afford it. This is a great way to also allow them to earn it. Based on that, do you think people appreciate the site more when they've earned their access rather than when it's just given to them.

ANDREW: Absolutely.

STU: So let's also quickly transition to talk about your pricing, because you have many different pricing options. You offer a monthly price, a quarterly price, and an annual price, but you emphasize the monthly. Can you talk to us about how you've set that up and why you chose to do that way?

ANDREW: You know, now that you mention it, I'm thinking maybe I should emphasize the annual. I'll have to play around with it. It's kind of fun actually to play around with the design and to play around with the flow. When you do, you realize that the same quality content, the same information, the same everything, can be more valuable and generate more revenue and more excitement if you adjust some little thing.

"...You realize that the same quality content, the same information, the same everything, can be more valuable and generate more revenue and more excitement if you adjust some little thing."

For example, we made the "Call to Action" button on the home page more prominent and suddenly orders went up. It's not because I improved the courses, it's not because I improved the quality of my recording or the quality of my guests, it's just I improved the placement of the Call to Action button and boom! – more people are now enrolled in the membership program.

So now that you mention it, we should probably try out emphasizing the annual option. The reason we put the annual there is I've always thought I want to charge monthly. That way I can keep the price low and I can see if people stick around. And if they stick around, it's telling me we're on the right track. If they don't stick around then it means that I have to go and figure out what to improve in the membership site.

We then added the annual price option (which is $199), we wanted to anchor the price. We wanted to make the monthly fee of $25 seem even smaller. And that's why we did it. And we also wanted to see if there was a portion of the audience that felt like the $200 annual fee was an insignificant expense. So we should probably start increasing our monthly and increasing all of our prices, you know?

That was my thinking on it. Most people still take the monthly but, as you've made me realize, maybe it's because we're emphasizing the monthly. Maybe if we de-emphasized the monthly option, more people would take the annual and maybe that's better for us in terms of overall revenue. I'll have to think about it.

STU: Well I think it depends. I think it's a good point, in that when you have a monthly membership, as you mentioned, it holds you accountable. It holds you accountable to fight every single month to win over your members again and again and again. And I like that sense of accountability as a membership site owner, because it keeps me on my toes.

A lot of people who sell annual memberships don't have that same sense of accountability to fight every single month. In essence, they get lazy with their content. They get lazy in terms of winning over their members every month. As a result, the overall membership begins to decline. Then they wake up one day and wonder where all their members went.

So I don't think it's necessarily a bad thing that you're focusing on the monthly because, as you said, it just keeps you accountable. At the end of the day, when you have a membership site, retention is the number one thing that all membership site owners should focus on. But unfortunately it's not. And so I like the way you're approaching that, Andrew. I think it's a smart move.

ANDREW: Well that's encouraging to hear.

STU: As we move forward, I want to give our audience a sense of how your site has grown. Obviously your site has grown tremendously with each new interview you add along with the number of courses that you've added. To help with that growth, you mentioned that you recruited some other people to get help with different areas of the business. You talked earlier about an editor, a course producer, and a researcher. How did you know who you would need to help you and how did you go about finding them?

ANDREW: I tried to keep the interview production really, really simple. I said I'm going spend an hour researching the person, I'll hit record and when we start doing the interview, I won't try doing any funky shots. I'm not going to do any impressive video and I won't do it live in person. I'm going to do it all on Skype, and then I'll publish it raw, and that'll keep things simple.

But I found that there were little things that I could pass on to other people which would free up my time to think about the rest of the business – not to mention keep me from burning out. I was really worried about burning out especially considering my production schedule of not just publishing a blog post every week but publishing a whole video interview every single day.

So I thought, the first thing I could do is get an editor. I can teach him how to edit my simple system and pass that on. So I did that. Then I thought later on I could use a little bit of help booking guests. So I found someone who could help me book guests. Then I thought, you know, the text that we use to promote the interview is pretty basic. It's the stuff that I say in the introduction to the interview. So I could hire someone to basically transcribe that, add a little bit to it, and then make that into a full blog post so I don't have to do that either.

Every little thing that I thought was going to burn me out, I would ask "Who can I find to do it for me?".

I found people by mostly by asking my friends. The video editor I found through a friend who talked about an outsourcing company in Guatemala. I said "Hey, are they good? Should I be using them?" He said, "Sure, go for it." He made the introduction and I went with them.

The virtual assistant, who helps me with booking guests and doing all these other things that go into the site, was introduced to me by a friend who said, "I'm using a virtual assistant who has more time. Do you want someone? It'll help me to be able to get her more money and it'll help you if you can use her." So I signed up.

I found those type of referrals go a long way. When I signed up for other online virtual assistant companies, they didn't really care about me. They didn't care about the quality. It just didn't work out. Now I go almost exclusively to my friends or to my audience when I'm looking to hire people.

STU: The other thing that I think is very important for people to realize, is that in the beginning, you were doing everything. You were doing all of your interviews, the editing, writing the copy, and getting the emails out to everybody. Now that you have more revenue coming into the business, you are investing it into the business by really building a team of people to handle specific tasks. In fact, you even have somebody – David – who helps you with some of the courses.

ANDREW: Yeah.

STU: In some cases, he's actually the one interviewing the guests. And that's important for people to realize, because sometimes we get hung up on our own egos to the point where, as you said, you burn yourself out. But by letting certain things go and realizing that as long as the people that you're hiring are trained and trustworthy, then the product itself will maintain its integrity throughout. Ultimately, that brings about more time for you to focus on the things that you want to do and it gives you the breathing room to do them even better. Would you agree there?

ANDREW: Absolutely. And charging for access to your site goes a long way to enabling you to do that. It means that you have a real business that other people can count on when they're trying to get paid. It

> "Charging for access to your site means... you can afford to pay for help and experiments."

means that you have money that you could afford to pay for things. It means that you can afford to pay for help and to pay for experiments. The membership becomes a dependable source of revenue. You know exactly how much you're bringing in every month and you can then count on it to grow your business.

STU: As we begin closing down here I want to ask about the things you are currently experimenting with. Can you share some ideas about things that you're going to try, add or subtract? Or just new things in general that you're going to do to enhance your membership?

ANDREW: The current thing I'm doing is just systemizing the membership so that it works flawlessly and predictability. That means getting the membership to the point where everyone knows exactly how many courses they could expect in the membership and I know exactly how much effort it's going take to do produce it. That's really important to me.

Going forward, I've been just looking at the emails that I'm getting from members and trying to figure out what they really want. People are saying they like the courses but it would help it they could get checklists to use with the courses. So I'm thinking now maybe we should hire someone to do a checklist for our audience for each course. What I'm finding is that when you take a course, you don't remember what you need to do. But if you have the checklist afterwards, you can go through what you've learned and use it.

I've also been thinking of doing a chat room or message board. I'm reluctant, and at the same time I see that it could be really powerful. So I'm not exactly sure if that's something that we should do but I've been thinking about it for a long time.

And then overall, we're always asking ourselves "what else can we do to get more members signing up?".

STU: Thanks for sharing Andrew. At this point is I'm going to quickly review what we've talked about and then I'm going hand it back to you Andrew for some final thoughts.

----- ANDREW WARNER INTERVIEW RECAP -----

Andrew really is a awesome person who has a lot of practical, real-world experience when it comes to membership sites with his site Mixergy.com.

Transitioning From Free To Paid Membership

Mixergy wasn't always a membership site. Initially he had hundreds and hundreds of interviews that he conducted every single week and he gave them away absolutely free. This was a huge site full of nothing but free content. However, although the site still has tons of free content, he transitioned to now charging for it. The way he's done that is to allow the content to be free for a week and then he archives it and, the only way to access the archives is to become a Premium member.

He also provides courses that teach one specific strategy in granular detail, and members have access to those courses as well.

The interesting thing for Andrew when he made the transition to charging for content was not only did his revenue increase, but so did his audience size. And the reason was, it created an urgency in his audience to go to the site at that point in time to watch and consume the content while it was free. Because those interviews are only free for a certain period of time, it created urgency.

So there is a very, very important lesson there for anybody who is giving content away willy-nilly for free. By creating urgency you actually get people to consume that content quicker, faster and it therefore creates more value.

> **"By creating urgency you actually get people to consume the content faster and it therefore creates more value."**

Initially, Andrew's approach to his site was a matter of survival. Meaning, if Mixergy.com could survive on its own, great; if it dies, well then it wasn't meant to be. So in the beginning to keep afloat, he was just charging for advertising. He had sponsors at the beginning of his interviews and that's how he was earning revenue. But when he transitioned to the paid membership model and began offering the courses as well, his revenue skyrocketed.

Now, there are two real things that Andrew is selling from within his membership. The first are the interviews with all of these well-known business experts and start-up founders and so forth. People get access to the archives of those. In addition, Andrew has begun to create specific courses that focus on a certain subject matter. They're more detailed. There's more step-by-step instruction. He uses GoToMeeting and really dives into the computer of the person that he's interviewing by showing them step-by-step what they are teaching their particular audience.

The reason he did this was his audience requested it. He was listening to his audience. That's one thing Andrew does very, very, well is listen to the needs of the audience. And they were saying "We love your interviews. They're jam-packed full of practical tips. But can you show us a more-step-by-step? More granular?". And that's what Andrew began providing his audience.

Test Your Ideas First

Before rolling his courses out, Andrew tested the waters first. He tested an idea for a course by first sending an email to his list. In that email he explained "I'm thinking about doing a course. It's going to be limited to twenty people. If you're interested let me know". Well the response immediately told him that they were onto something.

Although the first course was admittedly not the highest of quality (poor audio and video), Andrew advises "don't focus on quality. Don't obsess over it at first. Focus on quantity. Because when you are producing a lot of stuff, you're going to learn how to get better and better by doing. Focus on small changes that you can make and you're naturally going to get better and better instead of obsessing over it in the beginning".

Make It Easy For People To Find You

Andrew went on to explain that the more stuff you put out there, the more people will find you. That was certainly a big key to Andrew's success -

the sheer volume of content that he creates has helped him attract a much wider audience.

He said "Google doesn't distinguish between good quality and bad". So when you have all this stuff out there, naturally it brings in a whole bunch of different ways that people can find you. And he gave us some great examples including the one from Sex.com and the words 'I hate you' and how that played a role in his site.

Charge From The Beginning

Making the transition from "free" to "paid" wasn't exactly easy. Andrew admitted the transition was actually pretty rough. He had trained his audience right from the get-go to expect everything for free. And when he began charging, he got quite a lot of backlash from people who just always wanted access to that content for free. But a few people spoke up and they began supporting Andrew stating that if he charges for his site, he can create a higher quality product and he can spend more time it. It could therefore become a real business. At the end of the day, his site was about "building a business" so it made sense. Slowly but surely, his audience came around and now obviously it's a huge success.

So Andrew's advice on that is to "charge from the beginning if you can". Charging people for something is a skill and you can always make it better. Even if your first production is crap, he said: "You can improve it and give the people that invested in the beginning the revised version. Give them a better version for free". But always charge from the beginning.

> "Charge from the beginning."

Get Creative With Your Membership Levels

The way he protects his content is that he has two membership levels. He has the "Premium" level and the "Vault" level. He only sells the Premium level and that gives people access to all the archived interviews as well as the specific courses.

What I found interesting was that he uses the Vault level as a way to work with different people who may not be able to afford the particular Premium membership. Typically they contact him and say "Listen, I really love your stuff and would love to have access to those interviews. However I can't afford it." He says, "No problem. Perhaps you can help me out with this and in exchange I'll give you access to the Vault." So it's a very powerful way to get help and use the Vault level.

Focus On A Few Things

Another tip from Andrew was regarding your overall progress. He said when you are producing a membership site, realize that there are so many things that you can change and so many things that you can modify, but you can't get overwhelmed by that. You can't do everything. You've got to focus on a few things that you can tweak, and move forward from there.

He said at the end of the day, even with bad days and bad months, he makes more money every single month because of his paid membership. He said "value your content and start charging for it" because when you value it, other people give value to it as well.

A Unique Perspective On Pricing Your Membership

As far as pricing goes, Andrew has three options: monthly, quarterly and the annual option. On the salesletter, he focuses on emphasizing the monthly option. However, what I found interesting is the reason why. Andrew said he does this because it holds him accountable to produce great content every month. It forces him to stay focused on producing value for his members every month so that they'll stay. So for him, it's more of an accountability measure that prevents him from getting "lazy" with his content (which can sometimes happen for anyone offering an "annual" option).

Get Beyond Yourself

We also talked about the growth of Andrew's site. And with that growth, he's expanded his team so that he's not the one doing everything himself now. Since he has more money coming into the business, he's invested some of that money into hiring people to help him create even higher quality courses and content. He has somebody who helps him with editing. He has somebody who helps him produce the courses. He has a researcher. He has somebody who helps him book all of the interviews. All of this is possible because he now has revenue coming in from his paid membership.

He said the thing is, in the beginning he just focused on keeping the production value simple so that he could train somebody to easily take over those tasks. Now he focuses on the little things that he can hand off to somebody else that will free up more of his time to focus on what he does best. And he said when you begin charging, you can pay people for help. You can pay to experiment with different ideas because membership equals dependable income.

Moving Forward

Moving forward, what is Andrew focusing on? Systematizing his entire membership business.

He's also looking to get feedback from his audience as far as what other things they want - and obviously one of the things they mentioned was a checklist. So Andrew's natural thought was "could I hire somebody to help create those checklists?".

He has also given thought to possibly adding a chat room or a forum. That's something he might experiment with. And finally, focusing on different marketing strategies to get more people into the Premium membership.

There are so many golden nuggets contained within this interview and I highly recommend everybody go to Mixergy.com to see what we've talked about in action. Not only to access the free interviews that are available, but also to see how Andrew uses the free content to then move people into becoming a paying member.

----- END OF THE INTERVIEW RECAP -----

STU: Andrew, I want thank you very much for your time and I want to wrap up with a final question. What advice would you have for other membership site owners or for people who are thinking about starting a membership?

ANDREW: Two things. First, it's really easy to create good content that people will pay for. All I do is interviews. You can see that it's just me using video Skype to record and interview my guests and then I publish it on a WordPress site. Very easy. And the courses are just a GoToWebinar subscription that I use to record them.

I don't know everything about business. I of course don't pretend that I'm the guru of gurus. So I bring on other people and I ask them to teach what they're really good at. It's not that hard to create good quality content that you can put out there and charge for.

The second thing is, as I said in the beginning, don't be afraid to spy. Sign up for my newsletter just to see how I handle things. Click on the videos, just to see how I show my interviews and to see what you can copy.

Stu, I signed up to your email list for WishList Insider and I remember seeing how you'd say that you had this new Bonus Plugin that was only available for members this month. You went on to say that "next month it won't be available" and that people should go and grab it. After seeing that, I said "I'm going to try that". If it's working for Stu let's see how it'll work for me, and sure enough it worked on my site too.

So we learn from watching other people and we learn from being a part of other people's communities. Thanks for letting me learn so much from you and for being so generous and letting me, frankly, copy a lot of your ideas, Stu.

STU: Well I am grateful to you, Andrew. You're a great example of somebody who just puts into action what they are learning. And I love Mixergy.com. It's a wonderful membership site that I strongly encourage people to go visit it. Once again, it's Mixergy.com. You'll be able to access great interviews, but also, as Andrew said, sign up and get on his email list to see how he uses his content to drive his paid membership. It's a great example of everything that we teach..

So, Andrew, thank you very much for your time and appreciate you joining us here today.

Andrew Warner: Thanks for having me on.

Profile Information

Name: Andrew Warner
Website: www.Mixergy.com

MASTER #3 – THE COMMUNITY CULTIVATOR

An Interview With Jon Bard
From CBIClubhouse.com

STU: Welcome ladies and gentleman. My name is Stu McLaren, co-founder of WishList Member and joining me today is Jon Bard, the founder of CBIClubhouse.com.

Now this membership site is very unique because it was created for a very tiny niche. But even though it's a tiny niche, Jon has done phenomenally well to not only cultivate a community of thousands of people but to also turn that into a very profitable business as well. So Jon, welcome.

JON: Thank you very much, Stu.

STU: Before we get started, I mentioned that CBI Clubhouse caters to a very tiny niche. Can you talk to us about who it is that you're serving and what is CBI Clubhouse?

JON: Sure. CBI actually stands for Children's Book Insider and we've been in business since 1990, and for most of the time we were basically just a straight-up newsletter.

It is a newsletter for aspiring children's book writers. So anyone who wants to write a children's book can come to us and we'll give them the information they need to get started. We'll help them along the way with writing tips and then also helping them get published and market their book.

For all those years it was an offline publication. Now, we are online.

We've been online since 1995 – or actually really going back to 1990 with CompuServe and AOL - but we've been online since 1995 but it was purely as a promotional tool to sell subscriptions to out physical newsletter. However, with the advent of WishList Member, we were able to really reinvent ourselves and that's where the CBI Clubhouse membership site came into play.

STU: To give everybody and understanding, this was an offline newsletter that you have been selling for quite a long time, and then you transitioned and moved it online. Can you talk to us about why you did that and what was the thought process there?

JON: We came to the realization that the traditional newsletter model was dying. And it's dying for good reason. Content is cheap. The content is everywhere. And trying to get people to pay for content is awfully difficult unless you really, really have something unique or you are just a true marketing wizard.

We felt that we were sort of on the downward curve of a model. And so I began reading about membership sites as well as reading books like "Tribes" by Seth Godin (I'm a big fan of Seth Godin). These things certainly got my attention.

I came to the realization probably around the same time that you guys were launching WishList Member, which at the time we had no idea about, that the future is in community; that what people really will pay for is not specifically content but content within a framework, and the framework being community and expertise at their disposal.

> *"...what people will really pay for is not specifically content but content within a framework, and the framework being community and expertise at their disposal."*

It's essentially the ability to have a guru or an expert take you under their wing while being surrounded by other people who are going through the same adventure with you. That's valuable and that's something that people will pay for and will continue to pay for while telling their friends about.

In the beginning, the idea of the membership site was really to continue doing the newsletter. The newsletter is still the focal point of our membership, but it exists now purely in electronic format (PDF), and it is now part of an overall larger experience, which is the Clubhouse.

The Clubhouse is our membership site which has lots of content, but also has the opportunity to interact with us, to ask questions, and to form critique groups with other members (which we call Fighting Bookworms). We are Fighting Bookworms. Other Fighting Bookworms can connect together, do things, share ideas and even connect in the "real world".

What we really were able to do thanks to WishList Member was jump off a downward curve and leap on an upward curve. It was a pretty dramatic change for us, but, our members loved it. They were knocked out by it.

> "We were able to jump off a downward curve and leap on an upward curve."

It has also significantly increased our income and we did it in the heart of a recession so we absolutely know it was the right thing to have done.

STU: I want talk about the structure of your membership before you came online and after. Initially it was an offline newsletter and then you transitioned to moving it online.

Was there a difference in the way that you priced the offline newsletter and then when you moved it online, was there a difference in the way you priced that?

JON: Yeah. The thing about working within a writing niche is that it's a wonderful niche and the people are great, the subject matter's wonderful and there's not a tremendous amount of competition within this particular niche. That's the great part.

The bad part is, writers don't spend money. They are very price sensitive. I mean, when I look at some of these people in a Forex Trading market or Marketing niche, and they're charging $2,000 and $3,000 and

$5,000 for courses I'm shocked. If I try to sell something for $2,000, people would just drop dead! They can't even conceive of something like that.

So, we basically had to go for volume in terms of customers and not price. But before we launched the electronic subscription, the physical newsletter was about $27 a year.

Right now, there's two ways to become a member of the online site. You can pay for a year in advance at $42.95 or pay month to month at $4.49. Either way you look at it there's a pretty significant income rise for us on individual customers.

On the other hand, customers are getting tremendously more value with the online site than they were getting before with the physical newsletter so it works out for everybody.

STU: I just want to get clear on your pricing structure. Were you charging $27 per month for the offline newsletter?

JON: No, no, no! That was $27 per year.

What they were getting was basically, an email from us once a month saying the newsletter's ready to download, here's where it is, go and get it. That was just really as far as our interaction with them went unless we had come out with a new eBook or some sort of backend product.

Today, we almost have a daily conversation with our people because of the membership site. So as a result, the value being so much higher, that now instead of the equivalent of being $2 in change a month, it's $4.49 a month or, as I said, $42.95 for the year.

STU: Awesome. This is a really important lesson for everybody because you're going after a different strategy of a lower price point but a lot more people.

I know through our previous conversations that you have a lot of people in your membership with over 4,500 paying members. I definitely want to talk about the dynamics of managing a site with thousands of people but before we get into that, I also want to talk about how you are adding add a lot more value. Because as you mentioned, today you're doing more than just publishing the newsletter.

Can you talk to us a little bit about the different types of things that you're doing within your membership site?

JON: Originally we filled the site with a lot of content that was from our back issues because we had over twenty years' worth of content.

So when we added new content to the site it was in the form of an article or it could be a guest article from somebody else.

Now, we do a lot more video. These are quick videos where we collect questions and then we answer them on video. We also have a regular podcast where we interview other authors, editors and agents. We transcribe these interviews which then produces two pieces of content – a pdf transcript and then the audio interview itself.

I also like to do screen capture videos (using Camtasia) where I'll show people how to set up their own blog or how to create an eBook or how to use a particular site that's interesting. Or we'll visit a publisher's website and I'll walk our people through it. Camtasia videos are very easy to make and very powerful. We also publish a variety of eBooks on various subjects that our market would be interested on.

There's such a range of ways to create content now that it's really just a matter of finding something that interests people, and then presenting it in a multitude of different ways. And that's really what we try to do.

One thing to note is that there's a certain maturity level that a site will reach. Sometimes, you have to almost throttle back on the new content because people become overloaded with it. CBI Clubhouse has been completely online for three years now. So when we add something we try to make it really impactful and we try to let it stand on its own for a little while.

In the beginning we were just trying to overload people because we wanted them to go 'Wow!' when they got to the site and saw all the content. Now we are much more mindful about preventing "content overload".

"Now we are much more mindful about preventing content overload".

STU: You just mentioned a whole bunch of things that people get inside of your site and I know people listening or reading this interview will be thinking "Wow! He's providing all that stuff for less than five bucks a month!".

It really is a tremendous value and I can see how a low price point makes it much easier to over-deliver. Would you agree?

JON: Yeah, but I'll tell you my one concern with over-delivering and it's not even over-delivering; it's just the nature of the beast with membership sites.

If you have so much content on your membership site, it becomes trickier to develop backend products. In that, I could come out with a new eBook but my people will say, "what, I haven't even gotten through half of the stuff on the site. Why should I be buying more content?".

> "If you have so much content on your membership site, it becomes trickier to develop backend products."

You have to really rethink your backend strategy, which is something we're deep in the middle of right now. I think that's where perhaps webinars, individual coaching and mentorship programs come into play.

My only concern with having a lot of content is not being able to sell more things on the backend.

It sort of limits your ability to create backend content and sell it effectively. On the other side, my thought is "Yes, let's overload people. Let's make it a complete no-brainer."

My attitude is if you come to our site and you claim to be interested in writing children's books, even if it's just a peripheral interest, and you're not willing to try it for $4.49 based on everything that you see there, you probably aren't ever going write a children's book. So, it's okay. Don't join.

But we really want to just kick people over the head saying, "Look, you can't possibly not do this." That's our mentality and with our market it's worked.

STU: Let's touch on that because you mentioned you have a lot of content inside of your membership but yet, when you have a whole lot of content, members can get overwhelmed.

Overwhelm can often be a top reason for people cancelling, especially within the first month (ie. They don't know where to start). When there is so much content to access, they get overwhelmed and then they bail.

Can you talk to us about that and how you prevent that from happening within your membership?

JON: Yeah, and it's still a work in progress and it has more to do with the limitations of WordPress than anything else but we keep experimenting with a number of things.

For example, we have a little "Quick Start" guide that we send people when they join. We also have a welcome video and a bunch of other things.

But at the end of the day the reality is, it's not as easy to create a clean, organized, easily accessible content site with WordPress as it is with traditional HTML. It's paradoxical but it's just sort of the truth. I mean, there are only so many things you can do with categories and tags as opposed to physically creating separate standalone sections.

We're still kind of fighting with that. We want to have a lot of content and we want to show a lot of content to people who are coming there who haven't joined yet. But, we don't want to make people throw up their hands and go "My God, there's just so much here.".

So we have our ways. We use categories and we have things broken out but, it is a little bit tricky, simply because WordPress was meant to be a blog format, not so much a magazine content-site format.

But I think it's getting better and there are more opportunities available within WordPress to break things down so we just keep battling away.

I think that what you have to do on your site is literally use the language, "Feeling overwhelmed? Don't be. Click here". That is a word that people are going to say. We know that. That's an objection so we have to answer that objection.

"…use the language "Feeling overwhelmed? Don't be. Click here"… That's an objection. We have to answer that".

So, one of the first things people see when they come to our site is literally a little thing in the sidebar that says "Feeling overwhelmed? Click here". By clicking that it brings them to a video where we talk them down and into the Quick Start guide. It seems to work, but it's not perfect yet.

STU: I want to touch on a couple of things when it comes to the type of content that you've got within your site. Whenever you have thousands of different members within a site, you're obviously going to have people at different levels. You're going to have people who just have an "interest" in maybe writing a children's book and then you have people who have a lot of experience writing a children's book.

How do you go about deciding what type of content that you're going to deliver within your membership?

JON: We try to balance it as best we can but we also have the recognition that the majority of people who are coming to us are beginners. So we have to take care of them. We tend to use the newsletter, which again is a standalone PDF that you download from within the Clubhouse, for more advanced content or for more intermediate nuts and bolts writing kinda pieces.

We occasionally pull content like that and put it on the Clubhouse, but what we really want is for people come to the Clubhouse on the first page to see "Okay, there's a lot of things that speak to me. I don't know much yet but I can see where they explain it and where it's very accessible".

The people who've been with us for a long time, they know where to look for the more advanced content, for the market news and that sort of thing.

Again, it's also a work in progress. As I speak to you right now I'm taking a break from re-inventing and re-strategizing how we present our message.

The publishing world has changed so dramatically that we have to now think about how we can make it simple and make people understand what their options are.

Not to digress too far but very quickly, there's this notion with a lot of people in the traditional publishing world that the "end" is nigh. It's all over and the print book is dead and publishing is dead. But the information doesn't go away, it's just provided another way. That's why now authors need to think like an entrepreneur. It's about publishing your own eBook, your own app, your own print-on-demand book, and going out and marketing it, promoting it and then following up.

Writers are becoming business people and that's really the direction we're going to go. We want to make that very clear that no matter what level of experience you have, when you come to us we're going take you by the hand and we're going to get you published. You can do it yourself now and we're going teach you how to market it and sell and build a career.

That's the sort of thing that even advanced writers need to have their hands held on. Because they're not used to that kind of a new reality. So again, it's like everything in that I could use the phrase 'work in progress' for every question you ask, but that's the way it works.

STU: Well I think that's important for everybody because, a lot of people don't launch their membership site because they're waiting to get it absolutely perfect, and the reality is, you and I both know, it's never going be perfect.

There's so much that can be done to improve a membership site and I think that's a valuable lesson for everybody listening here today.

JON: You can't possibly predict what your issues are going be. I'll give actually a good meaty tip to people here because it's something applicable to anybody who has a WordPress-based membership site.

The number one nightmare that we had at the beginning, for months, was WordPress's built-in password recovery concept. If you've ever used it, you'll know that when you reset the password, WordPress sends you this incredibly ugly-looking generated password with exclamation points in it and parenthesis marks and all that. This freaked our people out.

I was spending days just creating new passwords for people and responding to them. Then I found a plug-in, which I'm going to absolutely recommend everybody use. It's a free WordPress plug-in called "Improved User Experience" and, boy, does it live up to its name. It basically replaces the WordPress password system with one that allows you to reset your password by simply sending you a link to a page where you can type your own new password.

> "It's a free plug-in called "Improved User Experience" and boy does it live up to it's name."

The minute I found that, I saved probably three hours a day of sending out emails to people. And it's worked ever since.

That's the sort of stuff I'm referring to. You never know what your issues are going be, but you have to just trust that solutions are out there.

Just launch. Just do it. And fix things later.

STU: That is awesome. I'm definitely making a note of that myself.

I want to shift gears a little bit and discuss one of the things that is unique about your site – the fact that you have built a community with thousands and thousands of members.

Now managing a site with thousands of members is completely different than managing a site with hundreds of members. Some things are the same but the dynamics of having that many members can certainly makes things different.

Can you talk to us about what types of things are different when you've got thousands of members and what are you doing within your site to keep it a community even though you've got so many members?

JON: Sure. Well, certainly one practical reality is the more members you have, the more customer service issues you're going have. Even with that password plug-in we just talked about, I still constantly get people with all sorts of things like "I can't log in", "How do I register?" etc. We're looking to outsource all that stuff because frankly I'm tired of dealing with it. But that's a good problem to have. The more people you have, the more emails you're going to get. That's just the way it works. That's probably the least glamorous part of it.

> ## *"One practical reality is the more members you have, the more customer service issues you're going to have"*

In terms of how having thousands of members affects the overall "feel" of things, it hasn't been that dramatic for me.

One thing is – and again it's within the certain limitations of WordPress – is that WordPress is not a social medium. It's not like setting up, say, a Ning site or something like that where it's all about people connecting with each other. It still has a certain level of 'top to bottomness' about it, meaning, we're at the top, we're sort of filtering out information to people and they can comment on it and go on the message board and talk about it. But there's really not a great desire, I think, among our people to spend all day on there, private messaging each other and setting up your own pages. You can't do that within WordPress without BuddyPress.

In reality, I don't think we've tried to build it into a social network. We don't want it to be that. That's a lot of work and it's not really what we're about. We're an educational site. So that actually makes things quite scalable.

That's one of the beauties of WishList Member. It's very scalable and in a lot of ways, the experience now and the experience three years ago for the individual user is largely the same. Of course, there's more of them and so there's more activity on the message boards and such, but it still has a nice "homey" feel to it. It feels like a little shelter from the rest of the internet and that's what we really wanted it to be.

STU: Well you guys do a very good job of cultivating that community and encouraging that.

You referenced at the beginning of the interview that you call everybody the "Fighting Bookworms". I gather this evokes a sense of pride and helps to create a real sense of community.

What other kinds of things do you do within your site to create that rich community?

JON: We have recently started profiling our members more. This is sort of one of those community site one-on-one kinda things that we just missed. But we've caught up with it.

"You have to make your members the stars".

You have to make your members the stars. Now if you come to our site you'll see we have a rotating image at the top of the sidebar where it rotates in and out covers of books that our Fighting Bookworms have gotten published.

So we feature our members by doing interviews, podcasts and video interviews with them.

When we first started, we tended to go out of the community more for interview subjects, which was fine because we attracted some big names in our industry. In the beginning we needed to have the big names to add credibility to the site. But now we're really starting to turn inward by interviewing our own people and making them the stars. I think that's really important from a social proof standpoint so that people understand what we are teach "works".

We also have a Shoutbox, which is a widget plug-in in the sidebar. This adds a real time message system where people can type in a message and it sits there for everyone to see. It may be a question or a comment. But every couple of days we get on there and answer people's questions that they've asked.

That's tremendous value considering they're paying $4.49 a month to then get expert answers to their questions. But again it adds social proof. It shows that people are active and they're interested. And it also shows that we're responsive to them. They're smart questions that people are asking and when newcomers come there they see, "hey this is a serious site". These are people who are really doing it.

We didn't have all that at the beginning. Again, it was very much "Hey, here we are; listen to us". But the way we're bringing our people in now is through that sort of mechanism.

The other thing that we're ramping up again is to do is more of a cause-related kind of program, where we're going to try to get behind a program for, let's say, children's literacy, and give our members something important to do.

We realized that it's important to give your folks some responsibilities. They want it. They want to participate with others but you need to give them the direction.

We're talking to some folks now but ultimately it will probably be something related to children's literacy and we're going to try to mobilize our members to get behind it. So I think that will have a lot of impact in terms of building community.

STU: Awesome stuff. I commend you, Jon, for all that you're doing, and I love hearing that, because I think too often we focus on a membership site because it's our business and our revenue stream, but the community is really the thing that drives all of those things and the more you create the community, the more time you can spend on mobilizing your members. Plus I think it will go even further to enriching the bottom line.

The thing is, the "community" aspect of your site is what really becomes the glue of what your site is all about.

JON: Absolutely.

STU: One of the other things that I noticed you do well on your site is highlight the current month's content in your sidebar. I think that's a really elegant way of reminding the members of the new value you've added to the site this particular month.

Can you talk to us about how you communicate with your members and how you show them all of the new content that you have added?

JON: Well the first point of content is when the newsletter is up and ready they'll get an email about that saying "Hey, come and download it".

Then, we'll also highlight some of the new content in those emails that's been up on the site and also highlight some of the more interesting threads on the message board. The key is, we give them direct links to all of that.

One of the other things that we're working on improving is creating more points of contact and then really making those points more efficient. Again, one of the beauties of WishList is that it does offer a lot of points of contact. You can control where people go after they log in, after they register, what they see based on their levels, and of course there's all the email broadcast functions and the generated emails that go out.

> "One of the beauties of WishList is that it does offer a lot of points of contact."

Right now we're really in the process of taking an inventory of all that and asking ourselves "Are we making the best use of that?".

When we send a message out – even if it's a lost password recovery message – we are now asking ourselves is there something in that message saying "Hey, by the way, did you tell your friends today about the CBI

Clubhouse? Here's a link where you can send a referral message to five people".

I think it's really important to use those opportunities and it's real estate we all have. The question is: Are you using your real estate to your best advantage? My honest answer about myself is "No, we haven't been".

> **"The question is: Are you using your real estate to your best advantage?".**

So we're going to go piece by piece through every contact point available to us and see what can we do to tighten our bond with our members; to promote backend products; to promote upsells; to highlight the new material and to overcome reasons for cancelling. These are all things that I think have to be done.

It's one of the unsung parts of WishList that maybe we don't nearly use enough to its advantage and that is all the contact points available to you. So you have to optimize them.

STU: Jon, I can tell you're a seasoned veteran of membership sites just by that response. A lot of times when we're starting a new site, we're so focused on the structure of the site in terms of the way it looks and what membership levels we have, the content, and of course the marketing.

But we lose sight of all, as you said, the little opportunities, the points of contact, that can have a big difference when it comes to the overall experience that a member has within the site.

As you were saying that, I was smiling, because I'm thinking 'Damn, that's exactly what we need to be doing more of as well!'

JON: That's the thing. And I think it's really more just about being an entrepreneur than anything else, which is, you never stop learning.

You never stop being a student.

You can't beat yourself up because you didn't know something a month ago that now you do. You just do it.

For example, what I've been doing the last month is I've been taking days off and absorbing myself in the work of Jay Abraham, who I think is just the genius of geniuses. I've been reading page after page and making notes. And then I have this notebook full of stuff to do as a result of it.

I periodically have to do that. I have to step back because I know one one-millionth of what I need to know. So I'm constantly trying to learn and I don't beat myself up for not initially knowing something.

That goes back to what you're saying about "just launching". You can't know everything. You can't have everything buttoned up and perfect. You just have to launch and learn as you go. Have the patience to learn on the fly.

The other thing I think is actually pretty important, especially for new people, is you need a thick skin when it comes to cancellations. Because the first few times that people cancel it stings. I mean, it's like knife to your gut! Oh man, it's almost like a personal rejection. But of course it's not because people often times tell us why they're cancelling and for the most part it's, "I thought I want to write a children's book. I don't really think something I want to do right now".

I can't argue with that person. I can't persuade that person back. I mean, that's fine. That's absolutely a legitimate reason to leave. And usually, 99% of the time, that's what it's about, it's something like that. It has nothing to do with you and oftentimes people are very complimentary, even when they leave.

Reality is, the more successful you get, the more people are going to cancel. It's just a numbers issue. And you have to be completely dispassionate about it. It's not a problem. Nobody possibly could run a membership site without people cancelling.

"Don't worry about cancellations. Just keep getting better."

So if I had one piece of advice beyond "just launching", it's don't worry about cancellations. It's fine. Just keep getting better.

STU: Well said, my friend. I remember the first cancellation I had from one of my membership sites. I was dumfounded. I thought "what's wrong with the site. I don't get it. I don't understand!".

JON: Yeah, because you get so close to it and you think that it's the greatest thing ever and anybody who wouldn't want to be a member is crazy.

People have perfectly legitimate reasons and we find that we tend to get our cancellations after the 1st of the month. It made us think about it. People just got their credit card statements and after looking at their credit card statements they're cutting out everything that is not absolutely necessary.

Those folks will sometimes share this with us and we'll give them a few free months. We'll say "Hey, if you're really committed to being a children's writer, I don't want to lose you. We'll take care of you for the next few months. We'll carry you". Those people end up being very, very loyal customers and they tell their friends. So, there's opportunity even in cancellations.

> "There's opportunity even in cancellations."

STU: You bring up a really good point, in that a lot of times we can take it personally that somebody's cancelling. We almost want to end the relationship with that person forever. It's like they slapped us in the face saying that, "Oh your membership's no good". But that's not really the way to approach it.

As you said, by reaching out and "being human" can go a long way and many times that person will come back when the time is right for them.

JON: Sure. And that's why it's important when people cancel not to delete them from your member base. Just move them to a different level. We have a different level we call 'hold'. We don't call it 'cancelled'. They're on hold because we expect them some day to come back.

> "That's why it's important when people cancel not to delete them from your member base."

The reason why you don't want to cancel them is because within WishList you have the broadcast email function. And so you can go back to those people with special offers. One of the things that we do is we sometimes just send them a gift. We say, "Hey, I know that you're not currently a Fighting Bookworm but we're still thinking about you and we hope you still want to write. Here's an eBook that you might enjoy". This helps just to stay on their radar.

Then when you hit the entire list op with an offer, you usually get a pretty good response (even from people who are "cancelled"). We brought a lot of folks back that way. So I think that's another thing: Don't look at these people as cancelled; look at them as temporarily taking a break from you. And keep them there, stay in touch with them and then give them a good offer.

STU: I love what you're doing there from a marketing perspective and I want to dig a little deeper.

Because of your experience marketing and selling your site for such a long time, can you share with us some other marketing strategies that you use to get new members? Then we'll talk about some strategies that you're using within your membership to keep people interested.

JON: Okay. First of all, we did have a little bit of an advantage – well a big advantage. Which is we had our original site, which has been online since 1995 – Write4Kids.com – and because it's aged and loaded with targeted content, it has search engine rankings that are hard to beat. I mean, if you type in anything relating to writing children's books it's going show up as number one.

That's a blessing but it was also a curse. The CBI Clubhouse exists under a different domain and a different server and it's a different thing.

If you're interested to see how we did they can just visit Write4Kids.com.

Ultimately, what we had to do is keep all the content on Write4Kids because we didn't want to lose our search engine rankings. But the home page of Write4Kids is essentially a referral page to the Clubhouse. You get there and it's says, "Hey, were you dreaming about writing a children's book? You've come to the right place. Check this out. Click here". Then you're brought to the Clubhouse.

That was the way we massaged that. It was a little tricky but we still get tremendous amounts of traffic from that, just purely from search engine rankings.

Then of course we do things like guest blog posts, and guest articles. Those can be very effective and absolutely work when done on targeted sites.

We've also experimented with using social media as a way to attract new members. We have ten thousand Twitter followers and we have two thousand Facebook friends. With that said, I'm coming to the realization that the social media thing is fun, but as a marketing tool it's on its way to being drastically overrated.

Social media marketing is a time sucker and I'm moving away from it but I'll probably try to just come up with a smarter plan to really make the most of social media without getting too in to the weeds on it.

Then referrals, which is an area that we really need to improve on. We're developing a reliable plan to get more referrals and to create more word of mouth by giving our people something to talk about to others.

Writers tend to be introverts and loners and they don't really by nature want to go out and spread the word about something they like. They kinda like to keep it to themselves. And so we're working on ways to make it easier for them to go out and tell the world about us.

Right now that's really how we get most of our traffic.

STU: Membership site retention is certainly the number one battle that most membership site owners have, and to me, that's the battleground that can make or break a membership.

So much focus is traditionally put on getting new members in but I want to encourage people to shift their focus to taking care of the people that have already joined your membership. That means focusing on retention.

What kinds of things are you doing within your membership to maintain interest and keeping your members part of your membership every month?

JON: Well again, the first thing that everyone has to realize is that there are some people that you simply can't keep because, for whatever it is you sold them on in terms of their interest, the interest doesn't exist anymore. There's absolutely nothing you can do.

But what you can do with those folks though – and again what we're going to start doing – is say "Hey, sorry we weren't quite right for you but I hope you enjoyed your experience. Who do you know that might like this membership? Click here to our referral form".

By doing this, you can still get something positive even when people are leaving. Otherwise, I think a lot of membership site retention comes down to involvement. One of the reasons we want the "cause-related" thing, apart from the fact that we believe strongly in children's literacy programs, is we want people to bind, not just to us but to each other. We want to create an environment whereby if they left they'd miss it. They would be saying to themselves "Hey, I had all these folks that I was working with on the Fighting Bookworms and we're doing cool stuff for literacy. I have a critique group there and all sorts of other stuff and I can't leave that".

> "We want to create an environment whereby if they left, they'd miss it."

So that's definitely I think an important thing.

Bind them to each other. Bind them to you.

We do our best to really be personal and even with all our members we're always happy to answer emails when people send them to us and we answers those questions on a Shoutbox. The more people feel they have a connection to you, the more they're going want to stick around because they don't want to lose that connection.

"Social proof" is also important. If your members are discouraged, even if they're at a stage where it seems like it's never going to work out for them, I think it's really important to let them know that other people just like them have succeeded using the information you're giving them. It's really important to let them know that because it gives them hope. And if there's hope, they'll continue to stick around.

STU:: Well, one of the things I also want to ask you about is your "CBI Challenge". Can you share with us what that is, how you do you do it, and the impact it has on your membership?

JON: Sure. It was inspired by Ed Dale and the 30-day Challenge, which I think is just a wonderful thing that he does. It's a fun internet marketing step-by-step program for newbies wanting to learn how to market on the web.

All we really wanted to do was give new people a starting point. When there is so much content within a site, even with our best efforts, it can be hard to always make it clear what path your members should take.

> **"When there is so much content within a site, even with our best efforts, it can be hard to always make it clear what path your members should take."**

The Challenge is meant to be a path. It starts at the very beginning of, "how do I come up with story idea?" and goes on to subjects like "What kind of children's book should I write?". The whole thing has twenty modules.

Each module has some articles, perhaps a video, a link to the message board where people can discuss it with others, and an exercise. It's all self-done in that we don't grade their exercises or anything. But it starts in the very beginning and then it goes to the last module, which covers "how to start marketing yourself once you've gotten your book published".

We tell people when they start with us go to Module 1 and start there. Take a week and just spend the time going through the modules. You of course can sample around the rest of the site and read whatever's interesting to you, but at least with the Challenge you've now got a path through the membership.

That has been pretty effective for us and it's been a really great sales tool because again it's sort of banging people over the head with value.

As far as other marketing elements go, I would encourage people to go look at our sales page. It's really worked out very well for us and converts very well.

It starts off with a little picture of a cup of coffee and is says "See this? This is a latte. It's creamy, it's frothy, it's delicious. It costs about $4.50 and you could drink it in about 5 minutes and forget about it. Now look at this:". Then we have the newsletter, the CBI Clubhouse logo and we have the CBI Challenge logo. Then we explain what each of the items are. We say "see these things, they'll help you get published and they cost about the same as that latte every month".

It becomes very, very clear in regards to the value right off the bat. Actually, in a number of our testimonials people rephrase the latte example back to us, so it's definitely something that's stuck with them.

Of course that's a standard marketing approach but look to come up with your own version of what the latte is. It just makes it easier for people to visualize the value you are offering. So for us, one side of the scale is a latte or a hamburger of whatever it is. The other side of the scale is all this stuff, including a course, training, expert help, etc. Are you kidding me? It becomes an absolute no-brainer.

STU: Certainly the no-brainer pricing, as we talked about earlier, goes a long way to making it an easy buying decision. You've certainly done that with all the content you've have within your membership site.

But I love what you're doing with the CBI Challenge. Giving new people a clear path provides direction. That's really important for membership site owners, no matter what level or no matter how aged your membership site might be. If your members don't know what to do next then they're going to feel lost and they'll cancel.

> "If your members don't know what to do next then they're going to feel lost and they'll cancel."

I think that's a really valuable learning lesson for everybody.

JON: It's certainly been something that people enjoy and encourages engagement. People will let us know how their progress is going; "I'm on Module 6 right now", "I'm on Module 10 right now". It gives people a feeling of a home base within their membership.

STU: Lastly, as we begin to wrap up Jon, I want to talk to you about some of the plans that you have for the future. Then I'm going to give a recap of everything and then come back to you for some final thoughts.

First, before we get to the recap, can you share with us some of the things that you're looking to add, subtract, experiment with or looking to improve within your membership site?

JON: I think for us, because of the low price point, the big push has to be backend products, upsells and generating more revenue.

Again, if we were charging $199 a month I guess I wouldn't be worried about it, but because we're not, we do have do what we can to increase the lifetime value of each customer while giving them something that they really need.

I mentioned earlier that one of the pitfalls of a site like this is when you're giving so much content it becomes very difficult to sell more content to these people. They've already gotten the huge mega-order of French fries and they're a third of the way through it. At that point you're not going to be able to sell more French fries at that point.

So, what you have to do is come up with things that complement the content inside your site. For us, and I think for almost any information-based site, what we've learned is that people really, really want personal attention and personal access to the experts within the site (and they're willing to pay for it).

We have a mentorship program that has been very low key, but it's going to become much bigger. People can, at various levels from low to high, gain real access to an expert who can take them by the hand as opposed to simply just reading the material on the Clubhouse.

I think that's the future. What people want is community but what they want even more is access to the guru. They want that expert. They want somebody who's got their back. So, a lot of our backend products will be focused along those lines. Whether it's individual coaching or whether it's an inner circle kind of group or through interactive webinars. It's going to be a lot more hand holding and personal attention. That's really where we're going now.

The other thing, just in general, is to just continually improve what we already have. Like I said, hitting every contact point, improving the referral system, making the site clearer to understand, making a clear path through membership, etc. Membership sites are constantly just a work in progress.

"Membership sites are constantly just a work in progress."

STU: Well, Jon, I want to thank you so much.

JON: Actually Stu, I want thank you. I've said this to you in the past but I want to thank you on behalf of a lot of people who had the opportunity to re-invent their business because of what you guys have done. The way you've priced WishList Member and the support you give and the fact that we keep getting updates, I just think you're really to be commended.

You've impacted a lot of people. And I know, we were able to jump off a dying curve and onto a thriving curve and the reason we could do it was WishList Member. So thank you.

STU: It means a lot to hear you say that and I really do appreciate it.

I'm going to give everybody a recap of some of the things that we've talked about and then I'm going to hand it back to you, Jon, for some final thoughts.

----- JON BARD INTERVIEW RECAP -----

We've been talking with Jon Bard, the founder of CBIClubhouse.com, which is a membership site that helps children book authors create their children's book, publish them and sell them.

Now, this originally was an offline membership, and it started way back in 1995 and transitioned to an online membership around 2008.

Content Is Cheap

In the beginning of the interview, Job boldly stated that "content is cheap." One of the things that he realized was that the future is in creating community. Creating a framework which people can learn and interact with others and go through that adventure with each other. He said the original newsletter itself just became part of the membership site. Now the community is really the glue that keeps everybody there.

Dealing With A "Cheap" Market

The tough thing for them though was that they are catering towards writers, specifically of children's books. This type of market just doesn't spend a lot of money, especially in a tough economy. To get over this, they priced their membership at a low price point. It's less than $42.00 a year or $4.49 a month.

The focus for them was not on a high registration price but more on volume. They needed to get a lot more people into their membership and they've certainly done that. They now have thousands and thousands of members that are a part of the CBI Clubhouse community.

Content Strategy

Originally they filled the site with old articles that they had from their back issues of their newsletters, but now they have a whole lot more in terms of content. The key is that they're providing it in different formats as different people learn in different ways.

Jon said, "we have articles, videos, podcasts and audio interviews, eBooks and reports." He said he even provides screen capture videos showing people how to do different things and use different tools. All of which is focused on helping his audience write their children's book.

The key here is they have a wide range of ways to deliver their content and they find out what people want, how they want it and then they deliver it to them.

But that comes with a warning. Jon said, "Yes, you can pack your site so full of content and over-deliver and over-deliver, but you can run the risk of a couple of mistakes."

"One mistake is having too much content."

One mistake is having "too much content". This makes it very tough to create backend products. The other thing is, too much content can also overwhelm your members – and overwhelm leads to cancellations.

There are a number of things that CBI Clubhouse has done to prevent overwhelm with its new members including:

1. **Creating A Quick Start Guide** – This is something that helps walk new members through the key steps for success. It gets them taking action right away.

2. **Welcome Video** – This welcomes new members and reassures them that they've made the right decision in joining this community.

3. **More Organized Content –** Jon and his team have worked hard to try to organize all of the content so that their members can find what they want and they can find it easily.

4. **Use The Language Of The Market -** The other key thing is Jon uses the "language" of the market. Specifically they have an area on their site that says 'Feeling overwhelmed? Click here.' They're answering the objections upfront of their members and they're giving them clear instructions on what to do next.

Managing Beginners & Advanced Members

With a site that contains thousands of members, it's inevitable that you'll have members with different skill sets. Jon's site is no different. They have people who are just beginning. They also have very advanced users. But he said the majority of their members would be considered "beginners" and that's what his site caters to.

They do have areas of the site where the advanced members know they can access more advanced content, specifically within the **PDF** newsletter that goes out each and every month.

Consider It A Work In Progress

At the end of the day, Jon repeatedly indicated that your site is always going to be a work in progress. He is always asking himself "how can I simplify the site? How can I make it easier for my members?".

He said one of the things to realize is that you can't always predict the issues and problems that you're going to have when you have a membership site.

One of the biggest headaches for him in the beginning was just the WordPress password retrieval process. It was a nightmare in the way that it operated and the types of passwords that it was creating for his members. This one issue alone caused a lot of confusion and therefore a lot of support. But there was a free plug-in that was available that immediately made Jon's life a lot easier. It's called 'Improved User Experience'. It saved him upwards of three hours a day of support, just with one simple solution.

Jon went on to explain that although you can't always predict the types of issues you're going to have within your membership site, be sure to look for a solution regardless because they are out there. The point being, don't be afraid to launch because of "potential" issues.

Make Your Site Scalable

Then we talked about the dynamic that he has within his membership site when dealing with so many members. The great part is that running a site with thousands of members is actually very similar to when they began with just a few members. The site is scalable so it's easy to grow. They don't have a lot of social elements that require more hands-on attention which makes his site easier to scale. Because of that, it really has maintained a consistent feel throughout it's time online.

How To Cultivate A Vibrant Community

One of the things that they do to cultivate community includes creating a profile for their members. This was a very important distinction that Jon made in that he said it's important to make your members the stars of your site. Feature them in a prominent location and make them the stars.

In Jon's case, they feature the books that their members are publishing as well as conduct interviews with their members. He said before they looked outside of the membership for guests that they could interview and work with. He said that was important in the beginning because they needed to get credibility. They needed to have some big names within the community. Now, they find a lot more of their people within the site for the in depth interviews and spotlights.

They also use Shoutbox, which is a method to collect questions from their members and a way for them to respond and answer them. By answering the questions, it shows the community that you're listening, that you're aware, you're there for them and that you're certainly looking to help them.

The other thing that Jon said that they're looking to do as far as cultivate their community is to really get behind a cause. He said give your members some responsibility. It helps mobilize your members so that they're

> "Give your members some responsibility."

there for so much more than just the content. They're there for each other and they're there and working together for a particular cause.

Communicate With Your Members

In terms of communication, CBIClubhouse communicates often with their members. They send an email to their members every time a new newsletter is produced and they then highlight content, hot discussions and generally inform their members of what's going on.

Use Every Point Of Contact

One of the things going forward that Jon wants to implement are more points of contact. Even with little things like the page redirects within your membership site or your lost password email. Any type of communication that is being sent to your members, whether it be spontaneous piece of communication or automated, be sure to look for opportunities where you can highlight other content, overcome objections, encourage referrals, and upsell different products or services. Look at all the points of contact and look for areas where you can improve.

Look At The Big Picture

Another thing Jon shared was the importance of taking a step back and looking at your membership site from a big picture. Often we get so close to it, and we're deeply involved in the details. At the end of the day you just have to launch your site. You're never going to have it perfect right from the get-go.

You Will Get Cancellations

Jon said that you've got be aware that you have to have thick skin regarding cancellations. Don't take it personally. Look at it as an opportunity.

One of the things I loved was Jon's description of his 'hold' level. They don't call it a 'cancel' level. Instead, they have a 'hold' level and they still communicate with those people so that they stay on the radar of those

> "They don't call it a "cancel" level. Instead, they have a "hold" level.."

people. In fact, sometimes they send them free gifts just to stay on their radar, and this certainly goes a long way to continuing that relationship - even if somebody cancels within their membership.

Marketing Your Site

As far as marketing goes, they certainly had an advantage with the fact that they had a sister site called Write4Kids.com, which was ranked really well within the search engines for this particular market. Even to this day they continue to use that site to channel people from the search engines to CBI Clubhouse.

In addition, they also do things like guest posting on other sites to help generate more traffic. One thing however that Jon did not agree with was the use of social media for marketing purposes. He believes that social media is very overrated from a marketing perspective and that the time would be better spent elsewhere.

The big thing that they're looking to focus on moving forward is generating more referrals. They plan to create more word of mouth by making it easy for their members to spread the word.

"Some people just won't stay, and that's ok."

Retention Tips & Tricks

As far as retention goes, Jon made it clear that some people just won't stay and that's okay. You can still use that as an opportunity by asking who do they think would be interested in this particular site? That was a very important little marketing message there.

He said also developing a common cause binds your members together. If they left, you want them feeling like they would miss the community aspect. The stronger the connection they have with you and the others within the site, the less likely they will leave.

Jon went on to say that utilizing social proof works well for retention. Show that your other members are having success using the content shared within your site. Showcase your members often and you'll find your retention will go up.

Another retention strategy Jon uses is the CBI Challenge. This gives new members a clear path of step-by-step instructions of what to do when you're at different points. It provides them a starting point to work from and people can go through the material at their own pace and along the way, they can discuss and share their experiences.

Conversion Tips & Tricks

As far as conversion tips and tricks go, one of the things that worked really well for Jon on his salesletter is they have the "latte" comparison. It makes it easy to see the value built within the membership and it makes the decision of buying or joining the membership a no-brainer.

Moving Forward

Moving forward, some of the things they're looking to do is to create more backend products to increase the lifetime value of the customers and to generate more revenue.

Now they're coming up with more complementary products and what they've noticed is that people will pay for more for personal access. People like having access to the expert who will help take them by the hand and they are willing to pay extra for that access.

So there has been lots of great information shared by Jon and I truly hope that while reading this you have taken some notes and action points upon which you can apply to your own membership – I know I have!

----- END OF THE INTERVIEW RECAP -----

STU: Jon, I want to thank you very, very much. As I was going through that recap I kept thinking, there are so many good nuggets in here and things that I can immediately apply to my own membership.

Now I'd like to get some final thoughts from you.

What advice would you give for people who are starting a new membership or who already have an existing membership to make it that much more successful?

JON: First of all I would invite any of the WishList folks who have questions or thoughts or need a little advice of their own, to go ahead and just visit the site, CBIClubhouse.com. Use the contact form and drop me a line. I'd be happy to talk to you. Also people who have joint venture ideas or anything like that. I'm always listening.

The key advice I think I would give is for people to understand what it is that you're really building.

What we mean by community. The metaphor that I like to use is 'gated community'. The internet is still this giant, sprawling, ugly, crazy city with all kinds of neighborhoods that you can't figure out and where you're constantly getting bombarded.

You're getting emails from everyone and everywhere you go there's information overload and social media this and social media that.

What you really want to create with your site is a respite, an oasis, a quiet place where people can go and get what they need. A place where they know they're not going to get spammed, because it's a closed community.

What WishList does very, very well is keep those unwanted people out.

One of things we do is when people sign up, we require their usernames to be their real names. That way people actually have to stand behind everything they post. You're not going to get just a lot of silliness and arguing and flaming when you do that. It creates a safe place for our members. It's a quiet, calm place. It's a respite from the rest of the world where they're surrounded by likeminded people.

That's why we give them a nickname. That's why they're the Fighting Bookworms. I highly recommend that people come up with a fun nickname that people will want to call themselves and create an image to suit that.

Create a nice, calm, quiet oasis from the rest of the internet where people will feel good about being. Where they'll take a break from their day to come there and look at the content and see what other people have posted on the message board and feel like they can breathe.

I think no matter what kind of material you're providing and what kind of community you're trying to build, keep that thought in mind. Make it a quiet, calm, gated community where people can take a break from the rest of their day. That will become very, very valuable. As valuable as the information you're providing.

STU: Well said, my friend.

I couldn't agree with you more. An awesome interview and I really do thank you, Jon. You certainly have a lot of experience with this and I really appreciate you sharing it with our listeners.

JON: My pleasure Stu.

Profile Information

Name: Jon Bard
Website: www.CBIClubhouse.com

MASTER #4 – THE TESTER

An Interview With AJ Brown From TradiningTrainer.com

STU: Welcome, ladies and gentlemen. My name is Stu McLaren, co-founder of WishList Member. Joining me here today is Mr. AJ Brown. AJ is a successful stock options trader who's taken that knowledge and then turned it into a very successful membership site. I'm very excited to talk to him because he has not only a wealth of knowledge in the stock trading industry, but he's also got a wealth of knowledge when it comes to running a successful membership site. So with that, AJ, welcome.

AJ: Hey thanks Stu. Thanks for having me.

STU: Alright AJ, so obviously you had a background in stock options trading. I want to know, how did you take that knowledge and then it into a membership site.

AJ: Brown: As traders we have to realize that we can't be successful going at trading as the 'lone ranger'. I don't think you can actually be successful at anything if you try going at it as a lone ranger, because the power of the Mastermind far outweighs anything we can do on our own.

So the power of that mastermind is so critical. In trading, it's even more important because when you see something you really need to get an understanding of the way the rest of the world sees it, because in the case of trading, what's right is what everybody else sees.

If everybody is jumping off the mountain, you don't want to just say "no, that's not right". When it comes to trading, you don't want to be jumping off the mountain either but instead you want to be the one doing something to profit from people jumping off the mountain.

So, the only way to get that perspective is from within a group. When you get a bunch of people around you that are like minded, they might look over your shoulder and say "hey, I don't see the same thing you do, and I see this". Then, maybe five or six people say "yeah, we agree with x, y, z, and not you". That's when you need to take a step back and say, "okay well then, if all of you are seeing a certain pattern I better adhere to that instead of going my own way or going down my own path!". The mastermind concept is the easiest way to figure out the shortest path from A to B.

"The mastermind concept is the easiest way to figure out the shortest path from A to B."

Anyway, I figured this out early on, and in the late '90's, I formed a group of traders that were going to all the seminars that were being offered in my area by all the different gurus traveling around.

I essentially just cornered everybody at one of the seminars and suggested we form a mastermind group. They agreed and I got everyone organized by simply sending emails to the group. We would meet, get all of our ideas out, and I would basically be the secretary or the scribe. So during our group meetings I would write down everything that was being shared. Then at the bottom of those emails, I would include some of the stuff that I was doing in the trading world. I'd share some of the trades I was making and some of the strategies I was employing. I did that religiously for almost three or four years.

Eventually, people starting taking a real interest in my little blurb at the end of these emails because my trading portfolio started to really grow. In other words by me actually writing down everything that we had been talking about, I began internalizing it faster than the rest of the group. That meant I began seeing success in the area of expertise I was trying to build. The proof was in the bottom of my e-mails to my group because they saw exactly what I was doing. That was powerful for them because they started to forward my e-mails to other people. My e-mails to my group members started to go "viral!".

Then I started to get questions in reply e-mails from people I didn't even know. That's when I said "oh my gosh, I think I have something of value here. Maybe I should start figuring out how to make this into a formal newsletter". Then I thought, "hey, I've got content that is good historically and evergreen, so let's put it into some sort of membership site".

STU: So let me get this straight. This originally started as an offline, informal mastermind that you were looking to create. Then, not only was this mastermind helping you understand what you and the group were learning, but you also began experiencing a great deal of success because you were holding yourself accountable by sharing what you were implementing and the results you were getting. Then because your portfolio was growing, people within your mastermind began sharing your emails to other people outside of the group. Because of that, you started getting questions from people outside of the group. Is that right?

AJ: Yeah, that's exactly what happened. If you take a step back, there are some key things to pick out from that experience.

1. **Form A Mastermind** - If you want to be an expert on a particular subject, the first thing you should do is form a Mastermind around that subject. You want to mastermind with like-minded people who are either at the same place as you or even slightly ahead of you.

2. **Volunteer To Be The Note Taker** - Definitely, definitely, definitely volunteer yourself to be the secretary because there is something powerful that happens when you are the one writing things down. When you take notes for everyone, you become the one who's processing the information in your brain and then writing it down.

3. **Take On A Challenge** – Take on a challenge in that field to prove to yourself that you're able to implement what you're learning. Then, publish your results so that at least the people around you can see your results as well.

Follow those three steps and you will eventually become the expert at what you're trying to master.

The other thing to note is that people can be weird about who they want to learn from.

> "People often want "X" but what they really need is "Y"."

People often want "X" but what they really need is "Y". So when you're marketing something, you need to first get them excited and deliver what they want. Then you deliver what they need so that they can start getting the same results.

That was a big lesson I was fortunate to learn early on. People want to see the results. That's what gets them excited. That's what makes the content go viral. That what people will share and that's what creates interest in me.

> ## *"People want to see the results. That's what gets them excited. That's what makes the content go viral."*

Once they are interested, then it's important to begin sharing the information that they need. For me, those were the tidbits that I was processing in my brain and in order for people to experience the success I was having trading, they would need to learn those as well.

STU: I think that's really powerful for anybody listening or reading this interview. Regardless of whether your new to membership sites or you're a seasoned expert, the key in your whole message is that your success began as a result of the Mastermind. For you in the beginning, it was a way to expand your knowledge and to learn from others. But then, it transformed into a situation where you were positioned as the expert. Plus, it gave you a chance to begin creating valuable content by sharing your success – which ultimately got shared by lots of other people as well.

AJ: Well just to sum that up, it really doesn't help to be an expert in something if nobody knows you're the expert!

STU: Exactly! So then let me ask you, at what point did you make a transition to formalize this into a membership site?

AJ: When I realized that I had something of value. At the time I didn't know anything about membership sites or marketing this kind of information. So I reached out to somebody who did. I reached out to a gentleman named Segovia Smith and I said, "I've heard that you're an expert at marketing information, can you help me?".

It's one of those things again, where often times you can't figure everything out yourself from a book. For faster results, it's easier to just partner with someone who has the expertise you're looking for or hire somebody who knows the answers.

If you do hire someone, don't just hire them to do the work but actually do the work with them and learn by doing. People try to learn subjects by reading books, and it's been proven over and over that books are only so useful. I would say that books are good for getting a foundation. But the real learning comes, I feel, by immersing yourself into it.

There are two ways to learn. You can do it by trial and error, which I have found is one of the best ways to learn but also takes the most time and can be awfully painful, both financially and in the waste of your time.

The other way that I like to learn is by "guided discovery". That's where you model somebody who already knows what they're doing. So again you're not just hiring somebody to get the work done. That's being very short sighted. You're hiring somebody to get the work done, and then, by doing it with them, you learn how to do it yourself

That's what I did with Segovia. I just made a point of stepping in his footsteps until I got to the same level as him. From there, I was able to take what I had learned and go in my own direction.

STU: Awesome stuff! So, at that point you're taking your information, and you're beginning to turn it into a membership site that you've hired Segovia to help you with. What kind of information or content were you delivering to your members?

AJ: At first it was "real time" analysis of the market. So at first we started delivering content that was not evergreen. In other words we were creating content where people would need to keep checking in with us in order to get the most up to date information. And that's a mistake I see a lot of membership site owners make. If you want to get people on lifetime continuity, you always need to have something fresh. And you might say, "well I'm in a topic that doesn't have fresh". I mean trading is beautiful in that everything changes every day - especially recently". Yes that's true but you have to make an effort to create content that is fresh and up to date.

> "We started delivering content that was NOT evergreen".

I've been through a number of membership sites where after three months you know everything on the site. There's been no fresh information. Taking a step back, it became obvious that if they took a slightly different angle, they would have a way of continually adding content that would give people a reason to come back to the site.

So that was the first thing we included in our site - a daily update of what was happening in the market. Then we'd put information in there like a short 'Getting Started' course. Then we started adding Tools.

That's another thing anybody can add to their membership site – useful tools for your members. Go pay somebody on 'Rent A Coder' or a similar freelance site to develop some Tools you can give your members access to. Something that will allow people to get from Point A to Point B, doing your stuff easier!

We now have thirteen or fourteen different Tools within our site. Our Tools are original and use industry standards or, they are Tools that do things better than other tools in the marketplace. So people will pay a premium to access those Tools.

The other key part of our member area which is different than a lot of membership sites in the trading area, is we put a place for people to communicate with each other. The social aspect of it! Because of this interaction within my site, I'm getting Retention rates that are way above average. For example, our members are staying eight months or more when the industry average is generally three or four months. So I'm almost getting two hundred percent, more, and that's because I've included these little pieces!

STU: I want to kind of press "pause" and come back to some of the things that you said here because there's so many powerful lessons for everybody listening. I definitely want to follow up on the Retention and the Community aspect of your site. But before we get to those, I think what you talked about with the whole "Tools" is a really powerful concept.

When you're talking about different Tools, you said these are resources to help your members do things easier. Can you give us a couple of examples of the types of Tools that you created for your market? And then also where did you go to find people to help you create those?

AJ: First you need to get very clear on the process people will follow in order to be successful at whatever you're teaching them to do. In my case, it was trading.

Now once you're clear on that, you know exactly what people need to do to go from where they are now to being successful at what they want to do (which is what you're an expert in).

The next thing to do is take each one of those "steps" and see how you can accelerate that part of the process. Often times, the answer is creating some sort of computer or even now Mobile App in order to do make that little step of the process even easier.

Once you have a general idea of what type of tool you're looking for, first search the web to see if there's something that already exists. If so, look at how you can optimize it or make it better because people will pay for the better, more robust Tool. If the Tool doesn't exist, guess what, you've got something original to attract people to your site.

STU: That's great. You mentioned you have thirteen or fourteen different Tools. Can you just give us a real world example of perhaps a Tool that you saw would help accelerate the success of your members? And then, can you explain how you went about getting that created?

AJ: So for trading, we use the Investor's Business Daily newspaper. Every day the Investor's Business Daily creates a chart containing of all the NASDAQ and New York Stock Exchange stock lists. There's thousands of them, and Investor's Business Daily uses proprietary parameters that they put in this table. And we use those in order to create our "watch list" of tickers that we want to trade. So one of the "steps" in our process is to take an index card and spending about 25 minutes a day scrolling down all these things, looking for a combination of parameters in this table.

"This created a perfect opportunity to create a tool for my members."

This created a perfect opportunity to create a tool because as soon as the Investor's Business Daily offered their newspaper online, I could 'screen scrape' the Investor's Business Daily newspaper and then using an algorithm to do this analysis in a matter of seconds. So it takes a task that would normally be 30 minutes and turns it into something that now takes a few seconds.

To get this created we simply went to RentACoder.com, eLance.com and defined very carefully what we wanted. The key with any Tool is to define very specifically what you want to have it done and how you want to have it look. To be honest, I'm not very good at that and I'll be the first to admit that I'm not good at clearly defining for programmers what to do. But I've realized this and I actually found it easier to hire a "middle man".

There are middle men out there who will take your idea, talk it over with you, and then brainstorm ideas that they can then take to a programmer. Then, they hire the programmers who would be right to create the project and oversee it's creation.

For me, paying that middle man is actually more efficient than me just hiring the bargain bottom dollar programmer. Of course once you find a programmer or two that can really perform, then stick with them.

One thing that I've done is gone to one of these freelance sites and posted a small piece of the Tool that I want to create. Then I'll hire the top three or four winners of the auction to do this little piece. I like to think of it as a "live project interview" process.

After they've finished this small project, you will have a sense of who is right to tackle the bigger tool you want created.

STU: This is a great example because you took what was traditionally a manual, time consuming process of going through the Investor Business Daily newspaper, looking at those tables and analyzing the parameters, and created a Tool that does it for them.

AJ: Yes! But before we go any further, let me just say this; if anybody is trying to be an expert, or if you're creating a member site around a different person who's an expert, make sure the Tools you're having created are the Tools that the expert would use. Make sure the tools you create are being used by the "expert" in your site.

> "Make sure the tools you create are being used by the "expert" in your site".

One of the most important things I have found is that if the expert in the membership site is using the Tools (and it's obvious to your members that you're using the tool), you're retention will go way up.

STU: That is a big, big lesson! The tools then become a win-win for the membership site owner because if you create Tools that you would use yourself, it will make your life easier and then it's naturally going to transfer to be a winning Tool for your members. Is that right?

AJ: That's a hundred percent right. The expert should be a user of whatever membership site you create. The other thing is if you can create a "community" where you have people discussing things, be sure to join in on some of the conversations and monitor what people are saying.

In my case, I am a trader first and foremost. I make a fortune trading. That's how I feed myself, my family, and my friends. Many people who don't know me may not realize that all of the funds that come from my membership site are put into a Foundation. So I don't make any money from my membership (which sometimes I regret because it's a lot of money!). But I make all of my money from trading. So if your expert is a user of that site will also be able to find out things by simply monitoring the conversations going on in the community.

In our membership we have a way that people can get into groups to talk about trading. We just use a Forum built into our member site. You can just get a simple plugin to do this. Then, give your members a template on how to communicate in the forum to get something accomplished.

Then you promise that at the end of their process, you (the expert) will come in and leave the final comment. So what we do is we have people discuss the trade that they're interested in.

We also give them a template on how to communicate with each other and what ticker symbols to use in order to properly share what trades they are interested in. The members then post their "possible" trades in the forum and get feedback from their peers in the group. At that point we come in and put in our two cents in (and it's very easy to give an opinion).

However, at the same time, these groups are literally doing all the work of finding good possible trades and handing us on a silver platter what ticker symbols to invest in. From there we simply have to pick from the cream of the crop.

So if you can create a process your members can follow in order to communicate with each other, and you give them a topic to discuss, you could easily come in and add a little value to the discussion your members are having. But you're also going to get extreme value back, in that if your members are properly following this process, you can use your community to save time on your own process.

It creates a synergistic link. And be open and honest to your members and tell them this is what you're doing. It creates this synergy between them and you and you'll be amazed at the positive impact it will have on your retention rates. It's all about Retention. This is the kind of thing that will get your members to stick.

STU: Right! One of the biggest challenges for membership site owners is keeping their members. You mentioned that you have a much higher retention rate keeping your members upwards of eight and nine months versus the industry average of three to four. Do you think the "community" aspect of your site is a big reason why people are staying?

AJ: I think it's a little bit of all of it. Some people definitely stay because they get wrapped up in the community. I would say according to my statistics, that's roughly about 20-30% of our members.

A lot of people get wrapped up in using the tools. The tools are some of the industry's best, and they just want to have access to the tools, so that's why they remain a member of our site.

Other people get great value from the information that we provide on a continual basis, because again, we provide some of the most up to date information. So there are many different reasons why people stay.

STU: I really hope people soak up what you just said. A lot of times we rely on essentially one pillar of information or component of our membership site thinking that "this" component is the main reason people are staying. But in reality, it shouldn't really matter why people are staying as long as they're staying. Our job as membership site owners is to provide them as many reasons as we can. As you said, in your case, they could be staying for the "community", the tools or it could be for the information. But at the end of the day, AJ, do you really care why they're staying?

AJ: No. I just make it possible for everybody to stay!

STU: As we move forward, I want to ask you about some of the challenges you may have had growing your membership site. What would you say has been the biggest challenge and how did you overcome it?

AJ: We began operating our TradingTrainer.com membership in 2004 and it has gone through different iterations as far as what we offer, the platform we use and all of that stuff. The biggest challenge we have now is that after all these years, our membership has become so large in that we have so much content that new people are overwhelmed.

So what became very critical for us was figuring our a way to properly organize all of this information so that it could be spoon fed or dripped to our clients in a way that they don't get overwhelmed. People can only digest so much at a time. Yes, you can prepare them as much as possible that they're going to be drinking from a fire hose when they come and be a part of your community, but if it's so much of a fire hose that you blast them across the room and against the wall, they won't want to stay.

> ### *"If it's so much of a fire hose that you blast your members across the room and against the wall, they won't want to stay."*

That's why over the last two years we took all the information in the site and put it into digestible pieces.

Here's a good tip if anyone is ever experiencing something similar. Instead of doing all this yourself, look to find some "star" members in your site who might like to help. Give them a free membership and have them sort through the information.

STU: So what you're suggesting is to recruit 'stars' of your community to help. Essentially, people who have a presence in your site to then help you with the whole organizational process?

AJ: Yeah! In fact, we had so much stuff inside of our site that people were actually telling us by opening up support tickets in our help desk and saying "I can't figure out where to get started!".

That's one of the reasons we created a "Getting Started" Guide. But then even better, when you start creating all of these tools, instead of giving new members access to everything all at once, slowly drip feed it to them. You can then create anticipation of "what's coming up" and guess what? You'll find by doing this, your retention rates will go up even more!

STU: The key for everyone listening or reading is that the more your members consume your content, the more likely they're going to stay. So, the easier we can make it to get started, to consume, for them to immerse themselves in the information and the community, the much higher our retention rates are going to be.

It's worth it to spend the time to think through the steps that our members should be taking as soon as they become a member. Ask yourself "what path do I want my members to go down?". Then start putting into practice the types of things you mentioned like a "Getting Started" guide. That's really going to help guide a new member become more comfortable, sooner, faster, easier, and begin consuming the content. All of which is only going to help in terms of long term retention.

AJ: Well think about this too, Stu, (and I might be dating myself here), but when I was a kid there was something very popular called "Choose Your Own Adventure Books".

The idea was, you would start on Page 1 and then it would ask you a question at the bottom of the Page 1. Based on your answer to that question, you would be taken to a new page. So if you chose "X", then you would jump to Page 100. If you didn't choose "X", you would go to Page 200. Every time you read this book, yes you would start in the same place but you would always go through a different ending. It was so awesome reading these books because you could read the same book for months and months, and always get to a different conclusion.

Now think about how you could use the "Choose Your Own Adventure" concept and apply it to your membership site. Most of the people coming to your site have different end games.

> "Think about how you could use the "Choose Your Own Adventure" concept and apply it to your membership site.".

You definitely want to make the "basics" available and everybody in our membership starts in the same place learning the foundations of trading. But then we actually have our content, not only drip fed on a time basis, meaning 'hey you're now part of this thing, and every week you're going to get something new', but we also give our members the ability to respond to certain questions and depending on how they answer the question, a new part of the membership site opens up for them.

What's interesting as the owner of the site is that we can see what ending they get to. This gives us insight into what content they find attractive and we can see what parts of the membership they've opened up.

I encourage people to get creative with your content and think about how you can use it to also learn about your members. You might want to think, "hey, I've got so much stuff and it's so broad but most of my people want to get to one end point". The question is, do they really? Or will they be overwhelmed by having access to all the information at once?

It's about segmenting your content and then making it available through all these tools and plugins that are now available for us.

"It's all about segmenting your content."

STU: I love that! I'm taking all kinds of notes here because I love the concept of not only segmenting the content and organizing it, but I love the concept of giving your members the ability to choose what path they want to take. I just think the experience of participating in that process and selecting what path they want to go down, is naturally going to make them feel like the site is more customized and tailored to their point of view or end game. All of this is only going to help retention even further.

AJ: It's a win-win. Let me pull back the curtain here. When you have these great Tools that allow your people to have a beautiful experience, of course you're going to have an admin panel where you can start to see where people are going with their path.

This provides me a lot of valuable information about our members. If everybody is going down a certain path, then don't you think that's where I'm going to focus the majority of my content?

Or, you might also want to look at where the dollars are going because sometimes you may have less people going down a particular path but what you might find is that the people going down this path are spending more money with you. So then you might want to highlight that part of your site because even though you have fewer people, you're making more money.

The Tester

It's just like Facebook. While you're having a beautiful time using all the beautiful tools that Facebook is giving you to share your photos, share your videos, share your likes, share who you etc., Facebook is actually using that information for a different purpose. As a membership owner, you should be doing that too. I mean it's going to enrich the customer experience, and it's going to enrich you as membership owner in being able to offer what the customers want most. This inevitably will also fatten your pocketbook (which is nice too!).

STU: Well and the thing is, is the more you know about your members the more you can cater to their needs. And I think that's the core message that you're really giving everybody here. The more you know, the more you can help them in the areas that they want to be helped, and obviously that's only going to lead to a much better retention.

> "The more you know about your members, the more you can cater to their needs."

AJ: I realize that there are some people listening or reading this that are like "money monks". Don't be afraid to admit that you earn money by doing this. If you're one of those people, make sure you are also doing what is profitable for you. Because in order to make your membership better, you will need to invest more dollars. And if you're not making more money to invest back into the membership to make it as best as it can be, you're going to be screwed.

STU: That's obviously one of those lessons spoken from somebody who's been at this for a while. There are always things that we can do to improve our membership sites and without the membership site being profitable, it's just an uphill battle. But when you've got money to spend you can go out, get more Tools created, hire people to help manage the site, spend more on marketing, improving the site and so all kinds of things to make that site better. That's just a great piece of advice. Thanks AJ.

As we begin to wind down I want to talk about what you're doing to improve your site even further. You talked about adding new tools all the time. You talked about your site going through different changes as you made the big change organizing your content and so forth. What are you looking to do now at this point to improve your site even further?

AJ: Well, it's funny because as you know, when I first started there were no platforms like WishList Member for creating this kind of site. There were no standards for this stuff so everything had to be custom programmed which was a nightmare. You have no idea Stu, how much money I have invested in member portals over the years. I'm almost embarrassed! I mean, we're talking in the hundreds of thousands, almost millions of dollars. And the truth is, now there are standard platforms, one of my favorite being WordPress. So one of the things that we're doing right now to help us prepare for future growth, is standardizing everything we use by looking at off the shelf platforms.

Everyone who works for me knows, I desperately want to avoid "custom" solutions. If we do have to create something custom, it's going to be modularized as either a plugin or a tool (like we talked about earlier). It's really, really important that people stay away from customizing things. This is just my experience, but you can keep your costs dramatically down by just using standard off the shelf solutions and following the boundaries that they've created for you.

By the way, most of these platforms today have so much flexibility in them so you can still be very creative by staying within the native constraints of the platform like WordPress and WishList Member.

We have so many members after all these years, and we have crashed so many websites, that's it's all about robustness. That and simplicity. Using things off the shelf, creates robustness. So that's one of the main key lessons, and one of the things that we're doing right now is figuring out how can we remove so much of our custom solutions and keep it as simple as possible.

By using these standard off the shelf tools, you'll be able to create an experience that your members are likely familiar with online. Remember, your members want to learn the content. They don't want to learn how to use your membership. Your site should be intuitive. I really wish this was a lesson we learned earlier.

"Your members want to learn the content. They don't want to have to learn how to use your site."

STU: I'm writing that down. People want to learn the content; they don't want to learn the platform! If your members have to struggle to find information or figure out your membership site, it's going to create frustration and they're going to bail. So as you said, want to make it easy, user friendly, simple. And it's familiar to other websites they're already used to, they will have a much better experience.

AJ: It's win-win-win!

By doing that, your members now won't have to go through a learning curve just to consume your content. At the same time, you're making a more robust website so that when you have thousands upon thousands of members, your stuff won't crash.

The last thing a member wants to do is to visit your website only to find that it isn't working or it's crashed. That will obviously lead to cancelations.

The other important part of this is that it becomes a lot cheaper for you to manage and grow the website if you're using off the box stuff. It's crazy when I think about it because now you can create an awesome membership site using WishList Member for just a few hundred dollars instead of tens of thousands or hundreds of thousands of dollars like it did when I began. Plus, the sites look better! So why… why not just do it?

STU: Right! The other thing that I want to touch on real quickly, because I hope that this didn't get overlooked, and that is the tools you provide within your site, can not be downloaded. These are Tools that people can only use within the Members' area. Is that right?

AJ: Oh, yeah. Yeah. I'm glad that focused on that. You do give people downloadable tools as well, but the problem with giving people downloadable tools is that you can't easily update them and get it to everyone who has downloaded it.

Put the tools in your membership and first of all, you're going to get continuity because you're going to have a hook. You're going to have a reason for people to stay in your member site. But second of all, when you want to make the tool better, you just make it better in one place and everybody gets the better tool.

STU: Thank you for clarifying that.

So I want to ask you about the marketing side of things, because I know you are very, very good at the marketing side, and we haven't even really talked about that at all. How do you get people to your site so that you sell them into the membership?

AJ: Now that's very much like the whole retention conversation, where the answer that we came to the conclusion was, it doesn't really matter how you retain them. You try a whole bunch of different things and you measure it, and by doing so, you realize that it's a little of everything and that each person has stayed for a different reason.

The same goes for the marketing. We do so many different things when it comes to marketing our membership. We use direct mail, radio campaigns, online marketing, banner ads, CPA campaigns [Cost per Action] and many more. W still have an affiliate manager and we do joint venture promotions. We do it all!

One of the things that I learnt early on was that you want to approach your marketing like a tripod. You want to be bringing in people into your member website with at least three different primary methods and you just focus on these three methods (especially in the beginning). That means if one of them fails, you still have two legs to stand on.

> "You want to approach your marketing like a tripod".

That way you only need to focus on getting three stable sources of incoming members established. From there you can start playing around with other sources that could replace one of your primary ones if they were to get shut down.

That's really the strategy we use.

As far as specifics, right now we're getting a ton of people from our radio ads. Radio is an amazing source for us because it's scalable. A lot of online sources, like Facebook ads, are not scalable.

"Facebook ads are not scalable."

For example, let's say on your Facebook ads you find that perfect demographic that buys and gives you the conversions that you're looking for. And let's say that during your "experimentation phase" you spent maybe five hundred dollars a week on ads. So once you found your winning combination, you're like "'great, we nailed it! We've figured it out! Now let's spend two thousand dollars a week in ad spend".

The Tester

Then your ad buyer comes back and says "well, we put two thousand out there but really there's only seven hundred dollars worth of traffic". So that's the kind of source that is not "scalable".

However, Facebook ads are easy and are perfect to do some research. We use Facebook whenever we want to research a new demographic or new product.

But with the radio ads, you can spend ten thousand dollars a week, or half a million dollars a week, and you will never get an end to the number of leads you can generate. The drawback with radio campaigns is, it was very expensive to get started and to get optimized. So there's a couple of different trade-offs between your lead sources.

So overall, we're doing a lot of radio ads and direct mail, bringing people offline to online. This has been very powerful combination for us.

STU: Another thing that you are very, very good is testing. You talked about trying a whole bunch of different things, seeing what works, and then analyzing what is bringing members in and what's not. But you're also very good at testing things right on your site as well. I know you've done extensive testing with pricing. Can you talk to us about the different price points that you have tested and what the results were?

AJ: Yes I'll answer that question but first let me just make a statement. That is, you are constantly testing things in your membership site and all the different things that get people into your site. If you bought some story that you could create a membership site, fill it with content one time and put it on an automatic drip system, and then walk away a rich man (or woman), then you're wrong.

A membership is constantly a work in progress. You're always testing or figuring things out. Earlier you heard me talk about how we are always looking at the path our members take and where people are winding up. We do that so I can continually add in the areas that are going to be most profitable and most useful to our members.

You are in this as a business owner which means you have to constantly test. There's no setting up and then walking away! I just want to make that clear for people who are listening or reading this interview. All the successful information marketers I know out there are fanatical testers. They test what people are consuming, and they test how they're getting people in.

So to answer your question Stu, we're constantly testing the messages people are receiving in order join our site, as well as things like pricing. In fact, one of our biggest tests we did was on our pricing strategy.

One of the first things we tested was the $1 trial. We heard other people talking about getting great results giving a trial to their membership site for $1 and then raising the price after 7, 14 or 30 days. That's definitely a model and I know people have had success with that. My results after fanatical testing for years on this, is... the dollar trial does bring in a lot of members but it also creates a customer service nightmare!

"The $1 trial does bring in a lot of members but it also creates a customer service nightmare!"

Our customer service becomes inundated with these people who are coming in on a dollar, and the truth is, not many of them stayed for us. I think somewhere between forty to sixty percent of them stayed for the first month and then they don't stay much longer. They're in it for the wrong reasons. They want to get rich quick! And maybe that's what you're trying to offer but we like retention, because we make more money in continuity than we do from one off customers.

So we then tried a $50 initial purchase. By the way, we have all kinds of different levels, but our most popular one is $99 dollars a month. So we tried a $47 trial, and that worked much better for us. The truth is, the $47 dollar wound up getting us the same number of leads as the $1 trial. We realized that people who were looking at the $1 offer thought that it was too good to be true and stayed away. So by raising the price to $47,

> "We didn't get any reduction in the number of people interested when we raised the price to $47 and we got rid of the tire kickers".

people immediately assigned value to it and said "okay, this isn't a scam! This is the real deal. I'll pay the $47 bucks!". So we didn't get any reductions in the number of people interested when we raised the price to $47, and we got rid of the "tire kickers" and instead got more serious people.

Then tried an upfront price of $147. So in this situation they would have to pay a $147 to get into our program, and then $99/month. Now, we did see a drop off when we raised the initial price to a $147 dollars. However, it was not a drop off of one third... or two thirds. In other words the number of members we were getting at the initial cost of $147 multiplied by the number of new members, compared to the number of people we were getting at $47 multiplied by the number of new members at that price, and we were making a ton more money offering it at $147. Plus, the retention rate went up.

Isn't that interesting? The retention rate went up for somebody who paid a lot more money to get in, than it did for the people who only paid $47. So currently we don't let people even into our membership unless they pay a $147 dollar acceptance fee. That way we get the real serious people.

The other thing it allows us to do, is create bundles. In this situation we offer my home study course and twelve months of our membership for the price of ten. Plus we'll wave that upfront fee. So this just allows you the ability to do some creative bundling.

STU: I want to quickly provide clarity there for everybody, because you're talking about all kinds of different pricing strategies and incentivized offers to get people into the membership.

When you are referring to the bundle offer, you're basically bundling different things of value that new people are going to get as an incentive for joining your membership.

You're also doing that with different pricing strategies, where they get twelve months for the price of ten, as well as different trial offers.

There are lots of great strategies people can try within their membership, but at the end of the day, as you said, it's all about testing. You've got to continuously test. This is not something you just flip on, forget about it and walk away. It's something that if you really want to get serious and really maximize the money that could be made within your membership, you've really got to test constantly and try different things. And what works for AJ may not necessarily work for you. But at least it gives you some ideas of things to try.

At this point I'd like to go through and recap what we talked about, because I've got a lot of great insights! Then I'm going to hand it back to you for some final thoughts.

----- AJ BROWN INTERVIEW RECAP -----

During this interview we've been talking to AJ Brown from TradingTrainer.com and obviously as you heard, he has a ton of experience when it comes to membership sites.

Mastermind Your Way To Success

AJ's experience actually started as a result of wanting to learn more himself. With his particular niche (stock trading), he said he knew right away that "you couldn't be successful by going at it by yourself".

He knew the importance of creating a mastermind and really getting a number of different opinions on what was happening in the marketplace. Since he didn't belong to a mastermind, he started one by meeting people at offline events and then staying connected with them by e-mail.

One of the important lessons from that experience was that he took on the role of the secretary. He would collect everybody's thoughts from each meeting, write up the meeting minutes and would then send that out to everyone in the group.

However, one of the things that he added at the bottom of these emails was his own recap of the trades he was making and the success he was having. Not only did it provide more clarity for him just going through the process of collecting the ideas, distilling them down, writing them and then sending them out, but it also helped him become more successful.

As he began sharing his results in the e-mails to the people in his mastermind, they began to share the emails with people outside of the mastermind group.

It wasn't long before that e-mail list grew and AJ began to get all kinds of questions from people outside of the mastermind in terms of the trades he was making and the success he was experiencing. That was the first 'aha!' for him in that he knew he had something of value. The question then became, how could I translate this into a membership site?

An important takeaway from AJ was, "if you want to be an expert, mastermind with others". And more importantly, volunteer yourself to be the secretary within whatever group you belong to and write stuff down. He said "you'll learn it faster, and it will help elevate your persona. It will help elevate your expertise". He said "send the info to the group because it helps you practice getting the ideas down into a clear format".

Another important insight from his masterminding experience once his emails started to get passed around was learning the difference between "needs" and "wants". In his case, people wanted to see the results that he was sharing, and that became the catalyst for the membership.

Hire & Learn

Once he realized that he wanted to formalize the membership site, instead of trying to learn the membership side of the business all by himself, he reached out to somebody who already had experience with that type of thing.

A powerful lesson from AJ here was that when you hire someone, do the work with them so you can learn by doing. He said, there are two ways to learn. The first way is through trial and error. That's very expensive and can be back breaking in many respects. But he said the other way, and the one that he prefers and recommends is what he calls "guided discovery".

"Model someone who knows what they're doing and do it with them. Hire them but learn it and do it with them".

Model someone who knows what they're doing, and do it with them. The key is to hire them but learn it and do it with them. Very, very powerful!

By following this strategy, AJ learned the membership side of the business much quicker. As a result, he obviously got his site off the ground and it's been very successful ever since.

In the beginning, the content of AJ's membership site started with real time analysis of the markets because in the stock options trading market, that's what people were looking for. So to satisfy their "wants", he was providing daily updates.

Evergreen vs. Up To Date Content

Contrary to what a lot of "experts" recommend, his content was NOT evergreen. AJ explained that one of the "hooks" his site has is the fact that the content on his site is fresh and up-to-the-minute. This was one of the main reasons people kept coming back and staying as members. He said, fresh content is very important for a membership site owner and we should never lose sight of that.

> "Contrary to what a lot of people recommend, his content was NOT evergreen".

At the end of the day, that's one of the things that people come to you for - the most up to date information. If your content is always evergreen, there's a certain period of time where new members will join, consume your content and then leave. Without fresh content, there is no reason for them to come back. So include fresh content within your membership.

Another tactic AJ implemented was creating and delivering a "Getting Started" course. This one piece had a profound impact on his retention.

Create Useful Tools

He then added tools and continues adding more tools to his site even today (he now has 13 or 14 different tools inside his membership). The focus of the tools is to help your members complete a "task" from your overall process easier, faster or more efficiently.

AJ suggested looking at all the different "steps" that somebody new to your niche will need to take in order to master what it is you are teaching them. Then think about how you can accelerate each part of that process so that somebody can become more successful, faster. By thinking through the different steps, and then taking each step and asking 'how can I accelerate this process?', you'll began to have all kinds of ideas for different tools that you could create.

AJ initially just searched the web for different tools he might be able to use within his membership. He was looking to see if there was anything already available that would could help his members at each step of his process. After finding some, he asked himself "how could I make it better, and how could I include that within my membership?". If there weren't any for what he wanted, he went and created them for his members.

A good example of a tool he created for his members was the one involving the Investor Business Daily newspaper. As part of his "success process", AJ recommended his members look at that specific newspaper because it had a table of the NASDAQ and New York Stock Exchange stocks. In addition, there were different parameters and symbols that he advised his members to look at and reference – that they would later use in their analysis.

So one of the things that he did was take that manual process of scanning, searching and analyzing, and he then automated it by creating a online tool that would automatically scan the Investor Business Daily newspaper tables and go through them to perform the analysis needed in just a few seconds versus it taking several minutes the old fashioned way.

One VERY important lesson from this whole "tool strategy" is that from a retention standpoint, one of the secrets behind successful tools is restricting access to these tools to members only. Meaning, these tools are NOT downloadable. By doing this, your members become accustomed to coming back into your site to use the tools and they then view the site as a valuable resource to their overall success. This will help skyrocket your retention.

I then asked AJ about how he gets these tools created. He said you can find people at places like RentACoder.com, eLance.com, and a variety of other similar freelance sites. But, he explained that sometimes it's just easier to hire somebody to work as a "middle man".

This person would help work with the coders for you and explain what you are looking to achieve. The reason for this is simple, sometimes coming up with an idea and explaining it to someone are two different things. AJ said "listen, I am good at coming up with ideas but I'm not necessarily the strongest at communicating that to a coder". So, now he hires somebody to help him work with the coders and take the ideas he has and put them into practice.

AJ then went on to say that when you find a good coder that you like, hire them outside of the actual freelancing site and work with them on a continuous basis. By doing this you'll save a lot of time (and money) creating additional tools.

Creating Community

Another important thing for AJ with the success of his site, was the creating of a "community". He said the community serves as another reason people stay in his membership. The key is to get people talking on the forums and then monitor the conversations. By monitoring the conversations, you'll gain so much insight as far as what topics are important to your members and what areas you should be spending more time on when you're creating content.

Another "trick" within your community is to implement mini mastermind groups. One of the things that he did was create a way his members could get into their own groups. He then gave them a template on how to communicate with one another inside of these groups. That was a very important lesson, because it's one thing to provide people an area to go, but it's another thing to give them a guide, template or instruction on how to make that whole experience the best that it could be. So by giving them a template the members can now come in, begin communicating, sharing and helping one another getting value.

One way to "plus" the mini mastermind idea is to jump yourself (if you're the expert) and provide an expert opinion. What's magical about this is not only does it give the members tremendous value but in AJ's case, his members are doing a lot of the upfront stock analysis for him (for his own trading) and he's able to come in afterwards and then give an overall perspective on what steps should be taken thereafter. So he said it's a synergistic win. The owner gets value, the members get value and it works tremendously well as far as retention.

Retention Strategies

When we shifted the interview to focus on other retention strategies that AJ uses, he said there are really three things that keep members within his site.

The number one reason people remain a member of AJ's site is for the "community". He said once his members get wrapped up in the community, they're hooked. Once they're connecting, sharing and engaging in a lot of conversation, the retention goes way up.

> **Top 3 Retention Strategies**
>
> 1) Community
> 2) Tools
> 3) Up-To-Date Information

The second main reason people stay is because of the tools he provides within his site. AJ freely admitted that some of his members only stay because of all the great tools that he's added within the membership. They use these tools on a regular basis but the only way to access them is within the membership – which is why people remain a paying member. That's a VERY valuable lesson.

The third reason they stay is for the up-to-date information that's provided within the site. Because the information is so current, they come to AJ because he distills all of the stuff that's happening in the market and gives them a summary of what they need to know (up to the minute) in order to make the right trades. In this case, if the information was "evergreen", it wouldn't be nearly as valuable – a very important lesson for all of us.

At the end of the day, whether people are staying for the "community", the "tools", or the "information", AJ doesn't care. As long as they're remaining a paying member. The big lesson there is give your members multiple reasons to stay within your membership.

"Give your members multiple reasons to stay within your membership".

Preventing Overwhelm

Now with all of that success, AJ said listen there are still a lot of challenges that he experiences within his membership. One of the biggest ones right now is preventing overwhelm.

Given that his membership is so mature, has been around for so long and has so many members and so much content, when somebody new comes in to the membership they can get overwhelmed. This prompted AJ to look closely at how he was delivering content to his members and what he realized was that it's important to sometimes slow down the delivery of the content to your members. Drip it out to your members and release it in digestible pieces so that they don't get overwhelmed.

If you have an existing membership experiencing a similar predicament, AJ said one of the easiest ways to begin organizing your site is to recruit stars within your community to help you go through all the content and get it better organized. He also recommended creating a "Getting Started" guide to help new members get comfortable as well.

One of the more creative content strategies that AJ uses goes back to his childhood with the 'Choose you own Adventure' books. From those books AJ has modeled the concept of allowing your audience to choose their own "path" through your site. So AJ has taken all of his content and created different paths that people can go down. He'll ask his members questions, and based on the answers that they provide, the site will send them down a different path. AJ explained that everyone has a different endgame and it's important to segment your content to allow your members to go down the path they want.

The other thing it does is provide you insight into what people want. When you start looking at the different paths people are going down, you can begin noticing different trends (ex. People who go down Path #1 stay longer that people who go down Path #2).

Focus On The Money

As a membership site owner, AJ said we all need to focus on the money, and you should never be shy about focusing on the money. He explained that otherwise, you won't have money to spend on improving your site. You won't be able to create a better user experience, you won't be able to create more tools and you won't have the money to update the site.

So with that in mind, you definitely want to be doing everything that you can do to enhance and improve your membership, increase conversions and retention and maximize the revenue that's pulled in from your site.

The Tester

Standardize Your Membership Platform

Standardize the platform you are using to manage your membership site. AJ explained that standardizing everything is really important because in the past he's spent hundreds of thousands, close to a million dollars, on different platforms and custom solutions. But he said it's very difficult to maintain a custom solution as you grow and it can quickly become very, very expensive.

So now it's much easier to keep your costs down when you use off the shelf platforms like WordPress and WishList Member. Back when AJ started, that just wasn't possible. But now technology has evolved so much that it's so easy to be able to do so much using standard platforms like WordPress and WishList Member.

He said you can get your biggest bang for the buck when you use these off the shelf products because it helps keep things simple by removing any of the expensive "custom coding". Unless it's for little things like modular plugins or stuff that you can take in or out, stay away from custom solutions.

Another key lesson when you're looking at the different platforms is to realize that people want to learn the content; they do not want to learn a new platform. AJ said that is a big lesson as far as creating an experience for your members that feels familiar and easy. You want your members feeling comfortable safe in the sense that they can learn without having to learn a different platform. Therefore design your site by modeling websites they are already familiar with – and WordPress makes that very easy to do.

Marketing Your Membership

When it came to marketing, AJ said "listen, we try a whole bunch of stuff to see what works. We do joint ventures, we do affiliate marketing, CPA, radio, direct mail, Facebook ads. We do a whole bunch of stuff. But at the end of the day, not all of it is going to produce profits". He said but you've got to try different things to see what works.

AJ has focused his marketing efforts on finding three primary methods to generate traffic and leads to his membership site. His rationale is, if one of those methods shuts down, they'll always have two others to keep the business moving forward until they find a third. He calls this approach the "tripod method".

AJ went on to say that too often people rely on one source of traffic. But that can be very dangerous because if that source, for whatever reason comes to a crashing halt, you're in very big trouble. He said right now for him, radio is working really well because it's scalable. It's very expensive to get started and optimized, but once you do it's very easy to scale because there really are an endless number of radio ads that you can run to generate leads.

Another reason AJ likes running the radio ads is that they are finding a much higher quality lead when they take people from offline traffic and then bring them online. He said this is very, very powerful and has proven to be very profitable for them.

Test To Maximize Conversions

As you heard in the interview, AJ is a fanatic tester. He said they're constantly testing different things. They look at what sources of traffic bring people in, what keeps them, where they have the best conversions and so much more!

AJ passionately warned all membership site owners that there should never a situation where you have a membership site set up to walk away and forget it. You should be constantly testing to find new ways to get people in, to find out what works, what conversion strategies are working best, what strategies are keeping people inside your membership, why are people buying etc, etc. He said there are an endless number of things to test, and you can always optimize your membership process in terms of getting new customers as well as your membership process for keeping new customers.

Price Testing

AJ has done a lot of testing, especially when it comes to pricing.

They tried the "$1 trial", and as AJ explained, yes it gets a lot of people in the door. However it creates a customer service nightmare. From his experience, he found the majority of those people to be freebie seekers and they didn't really stay for longer than a month but while they were a member, they created a customer service nightmare.

At the end of the day, the $1 trial wasn't worth it for him because he wasn't getting the high quality buyers that he was really after. What he did instead was raise the trial price to $47 dollars (with his regular monthly price being $97/month). He said this was much better and it worked just as well as the $1 dollar trial. The difference however was that he had a much higher quality member. They were staying around longer, primarily because people assigned a higher value to the membership. This upfront fee also helped him get rid of all of the "tire kickers" which reduced the strain on his support.

Another similar price test they conducted was raising the trial price to a $147 dollars. Now remember the monthly price for his membership is $97/month so they were actually requiring more upfront than the monthly ongoing fee.

AJ said this test actually produced much greater profits. Although they did see a drop in the number of people that were registering, it wasn't a third of what they would have got if they kept the price at $47 dollars. In addition, these members were a much higher quality buyer and therefore they valued the information more, they consumed it more, and they were a much higher quality buyer. So at the end of the day, they made a lot more money and those people were staying a lot longer.

There are all kinds of other things to test and AJ said they are constantly trying new pricing strategies to find the sweet spot of maximum conversions with maximum profitability. They are experimenting with things like "12 months for the price of 10", bundle offers (where AJ was offering a home study course in addition to the membership when somebody signs up) and much more. So, there are a number of different things that you can do but the most important lesson for all of us is that you've always got to test.

"You've always got to test".

Big Takeaway Lessons

There are a couple of things that I've really taken away from this whole interview especially AJ's approach to creating different Tools within the membership. That was a big one for me. The key thing that AJ emphasized, is it's most important to create tools that you, the expert, would use. If you're using it, then your members are much more likely going to use it too.

Plus, if you can also give commentary, and back and forth banter within your membership about using the tools, it will increase the likelihood that your members will have an interest in the tools and use them on a regular basis.

----- END OF THE INTERVIEW RECAP -----

STU: Alright buddy, well as we wind down I want to ask you, from your experience, what do you think would be valuable to know for somebody who is starting a membership site, or somebody who has already got a membership site?

AJ: Well I got to tell you, you summarized everything but honestly, we only scratched the surface. There's so much more to talk about.

Let me just say this. At my company (Trading Trainer), all of the people on my staff consider ourselves "Buckminster Fuller followers". Buckminster Fuller has a list of general principles that really apply to everything, and one of them is the principle of procession. That is, when you do something, when you intend and you focus on one thing, there are going to be things that happen at ninety degrees perpendicular to what you expected would happen.

For example, the focus of the honey bee is to go and satisfy his sweet tooth by sucking the nectar out of flowers. But by doing so, it just so happens that the bee gets his abdomen and legs covered in pollen and winds up pollinating all of our flowers - even though his primary purpose is to satisfy his sweet tooth!

So how do you apply that to your membership site? Just make sure that number one, you're clear on what you're trying to produce, and what you're trying to accomplish. Then analyze what's going to happen at ninety degrees.

You want to be focused on your intentions and be clear about your endgame. Sometimes, you may have to get into a mastermind to have other people help you see what your endgame could be. All of this applies to your continuity program. If you are clear on what you want to accomplish in your membership site and then you realize all these other things that are going to happen, you will then be that much more driven to get it done.

STU: Well said my friend. I just hope that people take the time to go back through this content because there were so many golden nuggets from this interview. Personally there are a number of big ideas that I can't wait to begin implementing in our membership sites!

I really do appreciate you taking the time to share with our audience.

AJ: My pleasure Stu. I love talking about this stuff.

> **Profile Information**
>
> Name: AJ Brown
> Website: www.TradingTrainer.com

ABOUT THE AUTHOR

STU MCLAREN helps business owners sell more by creating communities around their product, service or brand.

As the Co-Founder of the best selling membership site platform, WishList Member, Stu has a unique perspective on the dynamics of building vibrant (and profitable) online communities.

It's this insight that Stu and his wife have used to successfully launch a registered Canadian charity called World Teacher Aid. In less than a year, this charity has begun building schools and funding monthly school feeding programs in countries like Ghana, Kenya and Uganda.

So whether you want to make more money for yourself or raise funds for your favorite charity, Stu will show you the fastest and easiest way to generate recurring revenues by creating and selling your own products online and through membership sites.

WEBSITE: MyIdeaGuy.com
Twitter: @StuMcLaren
Facebook: Facebook.com/myideaguy

WISHLIST MEMBER
(www.WishListMember.com)

WISHLIST MEMBER is the membership site platform now trusted by over 30,000+ online communities and membership sites worldwide.

The reason for it's popularity is simple — it's a user friendly solution that within minutes will allow you to have your own membership site up and running, complete with protected, members-only content, integrated payments, member management and so much more!

You don't have to be a "whiz bang" techie to use it.

But if you are a "whiz bang" techie, then you'll love all the creative ways you can tap into it's API to create additional functionality.

To see all the features, example sites and to begin creating your membership site, visit www.WishListMember.com

---

WISHLIST INSIDER
(www.WishListInsider.com)

WISHLIST INSIDER is the membership site community for membership site owners. With thousands of members worldwide, you'll find a place full of tips, tricks and ideas for building a better, more profitable membership site.

Whether you come for the information, to exchange ideas with other membership site owners or for all the great resources and bonuses, WishList Insider has established itself as the "go to" place for anyone running (or thinking about running) a membership site.

Find out more by going to www.WishListInsider.com